# THE SPIRITUAL NERVOUS SYSTEM

## NERVOUS SYSTEM REGULATION FOR MANIFESTATION & WEALTH CREATION

EVA HATTIN

# CONTENTS

........................................

# MEDICAL DISCLAIMER

Any Information or guidance provided by Eva Hattin & Reading Bug Press is not a substitute for the consultation, diagnosis, and/or medical treatment of your doctor or healthcare professional. This resource does not create a provider-patient relationship and does not constitute or substitute medical, professional or psychological advice. Eva Hattin & Reading Bug Press are not registered health practitioners and therefore we do not provide a regulated health service. The content, advice, information instruction provided in this resource concerning improving your autonomic function and vagal tone in writing, verbally or in another format, believing it to be accurate, appropriate, and reliable at the time but we don't give any warranty of accuracy, appropriateness, or reliability. The information has been prepared in line with emerging research in this area. We do not guarantee any results this will have to improve your Vagus Nerve, Autonomic Nervous system or lifestyle. Individual results may vary.

Where possible, the information provided in this document is supported by external research. We don't give any warranty of accuracy, appropriateness, or reliability for third-party content. You should make your own enquiries into any research referenced in the 'Influenced By' section.

1. Any information or guidance provided in this book by Eva Hattin & Reading Bug Press is not a substitute for the consultation, diagnosis, and/or medical treatment of your doctor or healthcare provider.

2. You must not rely on any information or guidance we provide you with as an alternative to medical advice from your doctor or healthcare provider.

3. Eva Hattin & Reading Bug Press expressly disclaims all responsibility and shall have no liability for any damages, loss, injury, or liability whatsoever suffered by you or any third party as a result of your reliance on any information or guidance we provide you with.

4. If you have any specific questions or concerns about any medical matter, you should consult your doctor or healthcare provider as soon as possible.

5. If you think you may be suffering from any medical condition, you should seek immediate medical attention from your healthcare provider or emergency services hotline in your country (America: 911; Australia 000 etc.).

6. You are strongly advised not to delay seeking medical advice, disregard medical advice or discontinue medical treatment because of the information or guidance we provide you with.

7. Nothing in this disclaimer will limit or exclude any liability that may not be limited or excluded by applicable law.

8. Due to the nature of the content, you may be exposed to material that is triggering or otherwise psychologically distressing. If you experience distress at any point while reading or commencing the content in this book you should remove yourself from the trigger and contact your doctor or psychologist.

9.You should also make yourself aware of mental-health phone lines available in your area. If you are in Australia, you can call Lifeline on 13 11 14. If you are experiencing a medical emergency, call emergency services. If you are in Australia, call 000.

## Non-Disparagement

You acknowledge that we've established a valuable reputation and goodwill in Australia in the area of vagal tone and nervous system improvement. Subject to law and your rights in connection with the enforcement of this Agreement, you must not at any time disparage, permit or authorise the disparagement of us, any of our related entities or any director, officer, employee, agent, consultant or adviser of us or a related entity; or otherwise make, permit or authorise the making of any statement in anyway relating to or connected with any matters in dispute which is calculated or is reasonably likely to cause damage to us, any of our related entities or any director, officer, employee, agent, consultant or adviser of us or any related entity (including damage to their respective reputations). This clause survives termination of this Agreement.

## Exclusion of Competitors

If you are in the business of creating similar documents, goods or services for the purpose of providing them for a fee to users, whether they be business users or domestic users, then you are a competitor of Eva Hattin & Reading Bug Press. Eva Hattin & Reading Bug Press expressly excludes and does not permit you to use or access this book, website or social media pages, to copy or download any documents or information from its website or obtain any such documents or information through a third party. If you breach this term then Eva Hattin & Reading Bug Press will hold you fully responsible for any loss that we may sustain and further hold you accountable for all profits that you might make from such unpermitted and improper use. Reading Bug Press reserves the right to exclude and deny any person access to our website, downloads, services or information in our sole discretion.

## Dispute Resolution

You understand and agree:

You will contact Reading Bug Press immediately with any concerns so that they may be resolved quickly and effectively through friendly consultation: readingbugpress@gmail.com

In the event of a dispute, you agree to the following Dispute Resolution Procedure:

You must advise Reading Bug Press in writing of the nature of the dispute, the outcome you seek and what actions you believe will settle the dispute.

You agree to meet in person in Brisbane Australia or via an online platform, for example, Skype or Zoom, in good faith to seek to resolve the dispute by agreement and compromise.

If an agreement cannot be reached to resolve the dispute, any party may refer the dispute to mediation by a mediator appointed by Brisbane Mediations. This information can be found by contacting Brisbane Mediation.

Both parties must attend the mediation provided by Brisbane Mediation in good faith to resolve the dispute through mediation. Litigation via the court process may only be considered after a genuine attempt at mediation bought by either Party is unsuccessful. Confidentiality is paramount to both party's personal and professional reputations and standing in their business and community. At no time will any communications or discussions be made public. This includes but is not limited to any websites or social media platforms of either Party.

Any public discussion or comments about either party will be considered defamatory, harmful or otherwise damaging and will be the subject of compensation in any mediation or litigation claim.

Having a Dysregulated Nervous System can be the biggest blockage to accessing abundance and the life you have always wanted.....
No matter if you do all the steps, knock out all your limiting beliefs, and follow all the expert's strategies, if your foundation isn't strong and healthy, everything else won't hold up.

———

EVA HATTIN

# INTRODUCTION

It's funny how the concept of Manifestation seems to enter your life at the exact right moment you need it to. There seems to be a reoccurring theme I see when people share their stories and their first encounter with Manifestation and the Law of Attraction. Manifestation often enters our lives at the moment when we seem to be at our lowest or breaking point. When we have thoughts like:

- 'I have had enough of my current life situation.'
- 'I know there is more for me and I am meant for greater things.'
- 'I know I am meant to be living a life of abundance.'

It's like it intuitively knows that you are ready for it and it suddenly pops into your life.

For me, the concept of Manifestation divinely appeared in my life around three AM, on a Tuesday morning, back in 2018. I was up again, for what felt like the 100th time that night, breastfeeding and soothing my daughter while she was working her way through her four-month sleep regression phase (which really should be called the four-month brain progression - but that is a conversation for another time).

I was exhausted, struggling to adjust to motherhood and really just sick of the repetitive and what felt like dull nature of my day-to-day life. I found myself longing for any type of mental stimulation, conversations that didn't revolve around babies and the challenges of motherhood. I was longing for something for me as Eva the individual, not Eva the mother. I felt lost in motherhood. It was as if I was mourning my old self. Eva the Primary School Teacher, Eva the dreamer, Eva who was driven, imaginative, and content. It all seemed like a distant and hazy memory.

During the weeks leading up to that night, I had seen woman after woman as well as mother after mother on social media start and post about thriving businesses while they were raising their little ones. It looked amazing and something I could see myself doing. To be honest, I was incredibly jealous of their lives and how they cultivated a life where they could have it all - a booming business while being a mother. I was even jealous of the child free ladies killing it and wished that was me.

While I was breastfeeding during that warm summer night, I had the intuitive nudge to start looking at articles about ways stay-at-home mothers could make passive income and possible ideas for side hustles, something that I could do while my daughter napped. Just something for me - maybe a passion project that I could benefit financially from initially that would eventually turn into a business when my daughter was older. I was reading article after article when I was guided to a blog entry about the Law of Attraction and how it could be my saving grace.

That moment then led me down a long and amazing path. Like most ambitious women, I went on a self-discovery and healing journey...

- I consumed all the content out there
- read all the blog posts and books
- signed up for a few courses and webinars
- cleared some of my biggest emotional blocks and limiting beliefs
- experimented with all the different Manifestation techniques and strategies
- I tried it all!

It felt like I was back baby. I seemed to have found my perfect balance between being a stay-at-home mum while also challenging my brain and coming up with new streams of revenue that were looking very promising.

However, during this journey, it always felt like something was missing. I couldn't quite put my finger on it. It was just a feeling like there was still a missing piece to the puzzle I hadn't quite worked out yet. So I soldiered on using every free moment to explore and experiment with all things spiritual and Manifestation - trying to cultivate an abundance mindset. So far it was all very hit-and-miss.

Don't get me wrong, during that first 8 months or so, I manifested several free coffees and upgrades, an amazing business idea that was slowly taking off, a new $999 bed frame (they refunded me the cost - minus shipping - seeing as there was a delivery error), and my greatest manifestation that year was a random $10,000 cheque from one of my husband's relatives. I was on cloud nine.

Then it all seemed to stop one day. I couldn't for the life of me figure out why I could go from manifesting a $10,000 cheque to now manifesting more problems than desires.... unexpected bills, bathroom & plumbing repairs, cars breaking down etc. I was still doing the steps and strategies, I was still doing a lot of mindset work, and I was still throwing everything I knew at manifesting but it just wasn't working out like I hoped it would.

It was like I had come to a screeching halt and my manifesting abilities had done a complete 180. Looking back on it now, it makes sense why I suddenly seemed to have gone backwards all of a sudden.

We look for the Secret - the Philosopher's Stone, the Elixir of the Wise, Supreme Enlightenment, 'God' or whatever...and all the time it is carrying us about...

It is the human Nervous System itself.

———

ROBERT ANTON WILSON

# ONE

........................................

# THE MISSING PIECE

If you are familiar with the concepts of Manifestation and Law of Attraction, the works of Abraham Hicks or other well-known spiritual coaches and mentors, I am sure you will be familiar with the following sayings or buzzwords:

- to be "In Flow"

- in Alignment

- in the Vortex (Abraham Hicks)

- vibrating at a high-frequency

- high vibrational thoughts

- out-of-Alignment

- low-vibration or low-frequency

- deconditioning

- inspired & aligned action etc.

To me, every self-help spiritual guru out there seemed to be rattling off these buzzwords. Honestly, I found all these sayings to be a little 'airy-fairy'. They were these intangible abstract concepts, open for anybody's interpretation. There was no real substance behind them. Like I got the general idea of what being 'in Alignment' was but me being me I needed to know the specifics of it. I needed to know the exact concrete steps to take to be 'in Alignment'. Everything I came across in my journey so far was all very open-ended and idealistic for my liking.

8

What I also came across during the start of my Manifestation journey was that quite often these buzzwords were veiled in toxic positivity - I am sure you know the ones... 'You just have to think positively' (even when you feel like your world is collapsing), 'You need to be taking more inspired action to get there', and 'You need to be investing more in yourself and trying harder'. Sometimes these buzzwords are even mixed with a touch of shame, guilt or even coercion to buy products and services you don't necessarily need or want. (You know the ones... 'Buy my course now because it's the ONLY and RIGHT way to Manifest.)

I don't know about you but I am the kind of person who needs tangible evidence and information to process and work with such abstract concepts. I need time and space to explore and make sense of the complexities and nuances.

I decided to take a break in my Manifestation journey for a little bit after my complete 180. It all became too much. I used this break to catch up on some Netflix shows and sort through and declutter my house. This break was exactly what I needed and what my body was craving. A few weeks into my spring cleaning, I stumbled on a box of teaching resources that I had brought home on Maternity leave but never sorted/put away before my daughter was born.

And wouldn't you know, there in between the piles of resources, random stationery items, and literacy games was the folder I started curating on Emotional Intelligence and Childhood Behaviour Support. It was as lightbulb moment. It was as if the Universe was speaking directly to me... 'What if there is a connection between Manifesting, Emotional Intelligence, and Nervous System Regulation.' My two favourite worlds had just collided; Spirituality and Neuroscience.

I have always been interested in non-fiction topics for as long as I can remember. Even to this day, I much prefer to read about real-life topics than fantasy. This especially rang true when I started my Early Childhood and Primary Teaching degree. I became obsessed with brain development and how to best support my students with their emotional well-being. I have always believed and viewed education as a holistic experience, with mental and emotional well-being being the foundational elements to nurture and build upon.

You know, I don't know why it didn't come to me sooner. Most likely it was the lack of sleep thanks to #parenting. I flicked through the folder and got an intuitive nudge to look deeper into how Manifestation relates to our Nervous System. One of the notes I had jotted down was about how a lot of researchers refer to our Nervous System, especially our Autonomic Nervous System (more on that later) as our body's built-in guidance system or where our intuition and spiritual abilities/connection lies. There it was... the missing piece. 'What if the state of our Nervous System affects our ability to Manifest?'

From that moment forward, I used the time while my daughter napped to slowly map out how our different Nervous System States and their functions relate to the concepts of Manifestation and the Law of Attraction.

Eventually, I managed to take the abstract concept of Manifestation and make it tangible. I figured out a way to work with our Nervous Systems to enhance our Manifestation and wealth-creation abilities. I like to refer to it as "The Spiritual Nervous System."

Once I had the basics organised, I went about and looked at how other areas of Science, spiritual systems, and concepts like Human Design, Gene Keys, Chakras etc. can then also be mapped to and used to assist in regulating our Nervous System for Manifestation and abundance.

Now don't get me wrong, there is a myriad of other strategies and tips that help with Manifesting and working with the Law of Attraction. There are so many amazing, authentic, and knowledgeable Manifestation Experts out there that have systems and processes you can follow. But me being me, I- went looking for the foundational level. Most of their teachings focus on mindset and more "Level One and Up" topics and never actually touch on the "Foundational or Ground Level" work that needs to be done. Just thinking and working on your mindset isn't enough. Every cell in your body needs to be holistically aligned with your desires...

that goes for your Nervous System too. This explains why some people can have an amazing overflowing, positive mindset and yet they are haemorrhaging money left, right, and centre. There is a mismatch between their brain and body.

Like building a house, you need a strong and reliable foundation to build upon. The same goes for Manifesting. Having a Dysregulated Nervous System can be the biggest blockage to accessing abundance and the life you have always wanted..... No matter if you do all the steps, knock out all your limiting beliefs, and follow all the expert's processes, if your foundation isn't strong and healthy, everything else won't hold up.

This is the reason why I did a 180 seemingly overnight. For numerous reasons, I had unconsciously developed a highly Dysfunctional and Dysregulated Nervous System - I was living in my Survival Responses of Fight, Flight, and Freeze. I was exhausted, completely and utterly burnt out, 'Out-of-Flow' and 'Out-of-Alignment' holistically.

The amount of abundance, debt, and income we have is a direct result of our 'vibration' which ultimately comes down to what state our Nervous System is in. When we are vibrating at a high-frequency we tend to have a healthy and optimally functioning Nervous System. When we are vibrating at a low-frequency we tend to have a Dysfunctional Nervous System and are living in Fight, Flight or Freeze.

Ultimately, our Nervous System has the final say and automatically defines our mental state, emotions, reactions, and behaviours based on if we are Emotionally Regulated (in a state where we can effectively manage and respond to emotional experiences) or in an 'Out-of-Alignment' Survival Response State (Fight/Flight/Freeze).

How was I meant to be Manifesting abundance when there was a mismatch between my abundance mindset and my body being stuck in an unhealthy Out-of-Alignment Survival State? No matter how deeply and truly I wanted and desire my Manifestations, my Nervous System was blocking me and keeping me at a vibrational level where I was attracting "low-vibrational" things - bills, car breaking down etc. And really, Manifestation is about aligning our physiological, mental, emotional, and spiritual self to match our intentions and actions... and for a lot of people, we often don't know how to or even forget to align our physiological body altogether.

Throughout this book, I will walk you through, from a scientific approach, how to build a strong foundation for Manifestation and how to holistically align yourself via Nervous System Regulation. And guess what.... it doesn't take that much work. Especially seeing as I have collated everything you need to know and laid out the stages to implement them. All the exercises, "homework," journal prompts and rituals are simple. So simple that my 5-year-old does them with me.

Now don't discount this book and all the strategies if you are already a Manifesting Maven. I'm sure you are well and truly on your own Manifesting and healing journey and have done a shit-tonne of personal development so far. However, every one of us will eventually come to a point where breaking through to the next income ceiling or levelling up in life is a challenge. This may be because our Nervous System is blocking us as it doesn't feel safe enough to match our desired energetic setpoint, mindset or desires. This is where a little mindset work and some body-based therapies and exercises, which can be found in later chapters, can assist your Nervous System to feel safe enough to holistically align, match the frequency of your desires, and level up.

It's time to get started. Let's begin to holistically align you with your Manifestations and desires from the foundational Nervous System level up, shall we?

# TWO

..................................

# THE SPIRITUAL
# NERVOUS SYSTEM

To begin to harness our Nervous Systems for Manifestation and wealth creation, we need to understand what our different Nervous System States are and their functions. From this foundational understanding, we are then able to work with and optimise our Nervous Systems and environment so that we can spend more time in Alignment, develop a healthier and more flexible Nervous System, and experience more abundance in our lives.

The Neuroscience & Neurobiology of our Nervous System is complex, to say the least. It took me a while to wrap my head around the concepts and terminology. To make the following chapters easier to follow and understand, I will come at it come and scientific approach and have used the common names associated with our Nervous System States and put the scientific names in brackets e.g. 'Aligned & Regulated (Ventral)'. I have also diagrams, where possible, to help all my fellow visual learners. The first part of this book is theory and can be a little heavy so take your time. I have included a recap mid way with the key takeaways and summary.

We will then explore different strategies and tip that how all of this new information can be implemented in our Manifestation journeys in the second half of this book. I will walk you through how implement all this new information and create a 'Self-Care' plan to align your Nervous System to a higher aligned frequency. But before we dive in, I also wanted to touch on a few key concepts and clear up any misunderstandings.

**Stress:**

Stress is usually associated with our emotional or mental state but it can also relate to physical and/or physiological types of stress - think wear and tear of our physical bodies as well as our emotional and mental states.

**Regulation:**

Regulation or being in a regulated state is usually associated with being in a calm and happy state - some people even go as far as saying emotional regulation means experiencing no stress or "negative emotions." However, this isn't the case. Regulation is about having a flexible Nervous System that can manage and respond to emotional experiences and stress. It's about being able to identify, adjust and be in control of your emotions during a variety of situations. You can be sad and regulated; angry and regulated; excited and regulated etc. Having a regulated Nervous System means you have a healthy and optimally functioning Nervous System that can return to a Flow state more easily.

**Our Nervous System & its states**

In 'The Spiritual Nervous System', we will be specifically exploring how our Autonomic Nervous System and the Vagus Nerve affect our manifesting abilities and mindset. I wanted to make note that our Vagus Nerve makes up part of our Autonomic Nervous System and isn't a separate thing.

••••••••••••••••••••••••••••••

I am sure you have heard of Fight, Flight, and Freeze before. These are three out of the four Nervous System States we have - Regulation being the fourth. We move between all of these different states throughout the day. Each of these Nervous System States have a unique energetic frequency, specific emotions, behaviours, reactions and thoughts associated with them. As we move throughout these states each day, so does our energetic frequency or vibration which in turn affects our manifesting abilities, alignment, and energetic attraction.

When we are in holistic Alignment or Flow we enter into a high-frequency, emotionally Regulated State (Ventral Vagal- Parasympathetic). This is our calm, rest and digest, sociable state. Our Nervous System thrives in this state.

When we are Out-of-Alignment, Dysregulated we enter into one of the three low-frequency Survival Stress Response States:

- Fight (Sympathetic State) - Mobilising energy
- Flight (Sympathetic State) - Mobilising energy
- Freeze (Dorsal Vagal- Parasympathetic State) - Immobilising energy

These survival states all have their purpose but aren't the states we should be living in let alone manifesting from. However, the majority of people are living in these low-frequency states, have adapted to stress, and are trying their hardest to create their wildest dreams from a survival and holistically low-vibrational state.

In addition to these four main states, we also have two main blended states

- Play which is a combination of Fight/Flight +Regulation. We enter and use this state when exercising, dancing, and for amorous activities.
- Stillness which is a combination of Freeze + Regulation. We enter and use this state when we rest, meditate and relax.

In the following chapter we will explore what our Autonomic Nervous System and it's functions.

# OUR AUTONOMIC
# NERVOUS SYSTEM

•••••••••••••••••••••••••••••••

Here we go! Our Autonomic, or you can call it our Automatic Nervous System (ANS) as it works automatically or unconsciously, is composed of the:

- Brain & Brainstem
- Cranial Nerves
- Spinal Cord & Nerves
- Enteric Nerves - found in our intestines
- and the Vagus Nerve

Our ANS controls and regulates all our unconscious bodily functions. Things like:

- heart rate
- breathing rate
- blood sugar levels
- swallowing processes
- our organ's processes - liver, kidneys etc.
- gastric and intestinal processes (digestion and nutrient absorption)
- activation of our Survival Stress Responses (Fight/Flight/Freeze)
- and even plays a role in our reproductive health and fertility

It is essentially what keeps us alive. Our Autonomic Nervous System's primary function is to ensure the survival of our physical bodies. It will do everything in its power to keep our <u>physical body</u> safe from harm and can override our thoughts - hence why you can't solely think yourself out of a Nervous System State or think your way into abundance. Our ANS really has the final say in what Nervous System State we find ourselves in - *In Alignment or Out of Flow.*

Our Autonomic Nervous System is split into two main branches within our bodies: The Sympathetic Branch & Parasympathetic Branch - each branch having its own functions and states.

The Sympathetic Nerve Branch is responsible for our Out-of-Alignment Fight/Flight Survival Stress Responses. The Parasympathetic Branch of our Autonomic Nervous System is also split into two additional branches - the Regulated Ventral Vagal Branch and the Freeze Response Dorsal Vagal Nerve Branch. For my fellow visual learners, see the diagram below.

These two Parasympathetic branches make up our Vagus Nerve - Ventral Vagus being the front side of the Vague Nerve and the Dorsal Vagus being the back side of the Vagus Nerve. I told you there was a lot to it.

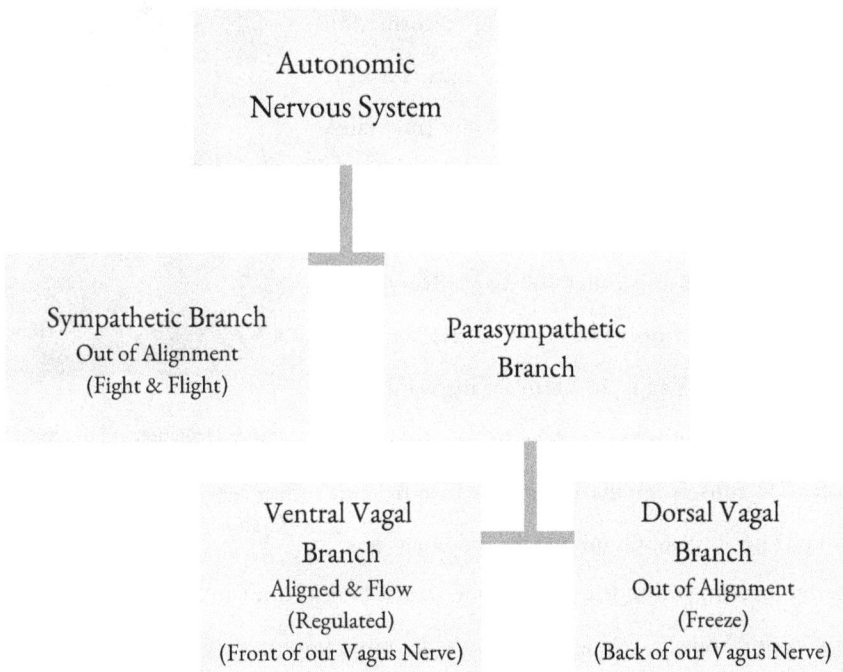

**Autonomic Nervous System**

**Sympathetic Branch**
Out of Alignment
(Fight & Flight)

**Parasympathetic Branch**

**Ventral Vagal Branch**
Aligned & Flow
(Regulated)
(Front of our Vagus Nerve)

**Dorsal Vagal Branch**
Out of Alignment
(Freeze)
(Back of our Vagus Nerve)

Still with me? Ventral Vagal ^ Alignment is the Nervous System State where we want to spend most of our time in.

# THE VAGUS NERVE

..................................

Within out Autonomic Nervous System we have a
nerve called the Vagus Nerve. It is split into two
main branches; The front of the Vagus Nerve
being the Regulated Ventral Vagus Branch and the
back of the nerve being the Freeze Dorsal Vagal
Branch. Our Vagus Nerve is the key to our
emotional well-being. It is the epicentre of our
mind-body connection - meaning information
flows to and from the brain via the Vagus Nerve. It
also helps us align ourselves holistically (mentally,
emotionally, spiritually, physiologically in
alignment etc.).

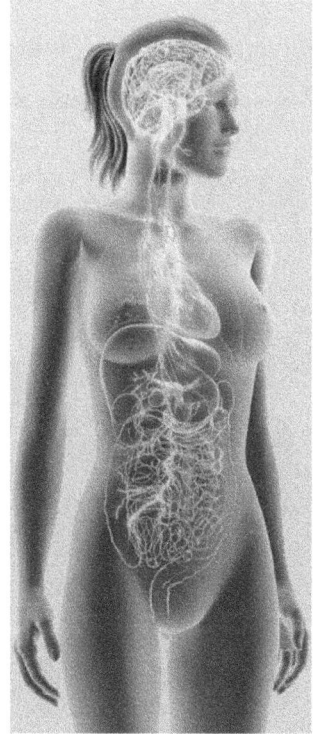

Even though it is called the Vagus Nerve, it is
a bundle of nerve fibres and is the largest 'nerve' in
our entire body. 'Vagus' in Latin means wandering
and that is exactly what it does in our bodies. It
wanders or runs from the brainstem in our skull,
down our neck, through our chest, abdomen, our

Image: Depiction of how the
Vagus Nerve wanders throughout
our body. (c) Science Journal
Photos

digestive system, and to the pelvic floor. It has connections to and influences every
organ in our body. The Vagus Nerve is the most important nerve to understand,
seeing as it is connected to and influences almost every organ, function, and
process in our bodies.

The Vagus Nerve has two "mind-body" roles:-

It plays a big part in transporting messages from our brains to our organs for all
those automatic bodily functions mentioned earlier.

- It is also sends sensory messages to the brain about what is happening or going on in our bodies through it's sensory fibres - e.g. signs of an infection, inflammation, change in breathing rate, increased heart rate etc.

The Vagus Nerves other main role is to move us back into Alignment/Regulation (Ventral State) after entering our Survival Stress Response States of Fight or Flight (Sympathetic State) via its calming Parasympathetic energy. Our Vagus Nerve is the key to unlocking our wildest dreams and most abundant life. It is the thing that enables us to holistically align with out wants and desires. The only catch is that it needs to be working optimally and feel safe enough to do so.

In a future chapter we will determine the state and health of your Vagus Nerve. I will also walk you though how to nurture and harness your Vagus Nerve so that you can move back into and spend more time holistically Aligned and Regulated...but I wanted to also mention the following...

Abraham Hicks often refers to entering the Vortex (or entering into Alignment) via meditating, napping, conducting breathing or grounding exercises.... all of these things are actually activities that related to the Vagus Nerve. When we conduct those activities, we are actually harnessing the Vagus Nerve's Parasympathic calming energy to help us move back into a Regulated, Aligned, relaxed State. Crazy right?! It does all come down to the state of our Nervous System and Vagus Nerve.

In the next chapter, I am going to walk you through the concept of Neuroception - the process of how our Vagus Nerve determines how safe our physical bodies are in the environment we are in and how safe out wants and desires are. When our Vagus Nerve feels safe enough to match our wants and desires we end up moving into the frequency that will energetically attract these. You will also begin to see signs and synchronicities that will enable you to easily take inspired action.

Your Nervous System cannot tell the difference between an imagined experience and a 'real' experience.

———

MAXWELL MALTZ

# NEUROCEPTION

......................................

Our Vagus Nerve determines how safe our physical bodies are via the process of Neuroception. You could think of Neuroception as our personal security system or even a part that makes up our intuition or inner knowing. It is how our neural circuits distinguish whether situations, places or people are safe, dangerous, or life-threatening - which then determines what Nervous System state we experience; Holistically Aligned/Regulated or an Out of Alignment/Dysregulated Survival Stress Response State.

Neuroception explains why we are happy to walk around a bustling park in daylight but walking through an empty park at night heightens our senses, we get a gut feeling that there is a potential threat of danger, or in general, gives off "bad vibes". This our Neuroception in action.

Neurception gives us access to information that we do not pick up with the conscious part of our mind. It works incredibly faster than processing conscious perceptions and thoughts. Hence why it closely linked with the divine, our intuition, and gut feelings/knowing.

Our Neuroception process is constantly identifying Signs of Safety, Danger or threats for us in three ways:

Signs from inside our body (Interoception)

The Vagus Nerve is looking for things like changes in heart rate; changes in our breathing rates or rhythm; what's happening within our muscles (tension etc.); our digestion processes (is it slowing down at all?); any pain, signs of inflammation, and even signs of dehydration. Examples of Interoceptive signs:

1. heart rate changes when we are on theme park rides

2. the contraction of our muscles when we jump out of fear

3. holding our breath when we witness and accident in progress etc.

## Signs from our external world (Exteroception)

The Vagus Nerve is looking for signs like high-frequency sounds; low-frequency sounds; unusual silence; unexpected noises like cars backfiring; unpredictable or unexpected motions - e.g. a bird flying straight at you; temperature changes; bright lights; certain smells, and anything else we can experience through our five senses. Exteroceptive signs can be within our immediate physical location, within our neighbourhood, and can branch out to national or global environments.

## Signs between others both humans and animals.

The Vagus Nerve is looking for signs like changes in facial expressions or even specific facial expressions; body language changes; tone of voice etc. An example of this type of Neuroceptive sign can be when you get a "bad vibe" from a person based on their body language or facial expressions etc. Another example of this is when you get the feeling that you're being watched. Your Vagus Nerve has picked up on something you are not consciously aware of at that moment.

.....................................

Our Nervous System sort of acts like a balance scale. If our Autonomic Nervous System determines, via Neuroception, that there are more signs of Safety than Danger in our environment, we remain in our Aligned Regulated State (Ventral).

However, if it determines that there are more signs of Danger than there are of Safety, it sends out a message that where we are, who we are with, or the situation we are in is dangerous and/or possibly life-threatening. When this happens we are <u>automatically pushed</u> into one of our Out-of-Alignment Survival Stress Responses (Fight/Flight/Freeze) and into a low-frequency state.

Neuroception is constantly looking for and assessing risks; looking for signs of Safety, signs of Danger, and signs of Life-threatening Danger. It's important to note that this all occurs below conscious thought and that our Nervous Systems can't tell the difference between getting ready to fight/flee a lion vs. getting emotionally overwhelmed due to stress and/or lack of sleep.

It just noticed changes in our physical body, different to those we exhibit when we are in our Aligned Regulated (Ventral) state, and therefore there must be a danger to us somewhere to have caused these changes.

Our brain/mindset doesn't determine if we are safe... it's our Nervous System that determines this based on Neuroception. It has the ultimate say. This is why we can't solely think our way out of or into situations, emotions, and abundance.

....................................

**Instinctively we all have two danger cues:**

- **High-frequency sounds.** This implies there is some form of distress happening. Our natural response tends to be trying to find or look towards the source of the high-frequency sound - e.g. trying to figure out the location of someone screaming.

- **Low-frequency sounds.** These sounds tell our Nervous System that there are possibly predators around and for us to get to the safety of the sounds that fall into the human voice range. We all feel really uncomfortable in situations with low-frequency sounds. Animals like elephants emit low-frequency sounds – so do severe weather patterns, avalanches and earthquakes.

All our other Danger and Safety Signs have been constructed throughout our lives and our ancestors lives (via Epigenetics) through the experiences we/they have had. Each person will have their own unique set of Safety and Danger cues.

For example, dogs are a Sign of Safety for some. However, for someone who has experienced a dog bite, to their Nervous System - dogs are a Sign of Danger.

Loud noises to you may feel like a threat or danger; yelling and screaming may remind you of some form of danger you faced in childhood or maybe an experience you had as an adult. Loud noises for others may feel calming and regulating; loud festival music, and sounds of machinery may remind you of fun and enjoyable experiences etc.

Being in crowds and around people may remind you of happy and fun social situations. For others, their history makes large crowds and lots of movement dysregulating - especially for some people who may have PTSD.

Now sometimes our Neuroception, and its ability to determine Safety and Danger cues can be a little faulty. It can cause us to react to a safe situation as if it were dangerous and vice versa; we could be in a dangerous situation but our Nervous System thinks we are relatively safe because it hasn't pick up and Neuroceptive signs to say otherwise.

There can be countless reasons for faulty Neuroception. Sometimes we may react to a certain stimulus because it is related to childhood traumas, a traumatic experience we had or a past relationship experience.

Our brains are organized to reflect everything we know in our environment – everything we are exposed to via our life, past lives, and/or the lives of our ancestors via Epigenetics (Genetic changes to our DNA) in the form of an experience or knowledge, is stored in the brain's synaptic connections from birth. This means all the experiences we have had or that have been passed down via Epigenetics and past lives are configured, wired, or imprinted in the structures of the brain and sorted into signs of Safety & Danger.

We might be feeling perfectly normal and then suddenly be triggered by something that reminds us of a traumatic event in our past or relatives past - reacting to this memory as if it were happening in the present time. We might not actually be threatened or in danger, but our Nervous System may be stuck in the past – ready to Fight, Flee or Freeze.

Our Neuroception can become a little faulty for other reasons too- if we are in a state of shock; severely sleep deprived; in pain, hungry; overstimulated/ experiencing sensory overload; or in highly emotional settings etc...

Getting out the door in the morning can be perceived as a sign of Danger. So can relaxing, slowing down or meditating, if we have been living in constant Out-of-Alignment Fight/Flight Stress State. This is because the physical changes when we slow down are different to our baseline state of stress where we are constantly wired and on the go. So if you hate the thought or feeling of meditating, it can possibly be because your Nervous System sees it as a threat to your survival. I have included a few tips and tricks to help with this towards the end of the book.

Thanks to Neuroplasticity, the brains ability to rewire itself, we can recalibrate our Safety and Danger signs so that our Neuroception functions better and we find ourselves living more in an Aligned/Regulated/Flow State.

..................................

Now that we have worked through how our Autonomic Nervous System/Vagus Nerve determines Safety and Danger, we are going to explore how that influences our Nervous System States. Each day we automatically move between several Nervous System States. The keyword being: automatically. Our brain doesn't choose the Nervous System state we find ourselves in. - It's our Nervous System moving us into and between these states to ensure our physical body's survival. The four main states we move through each day are the:

- Aligned/Regulated State (Parasympathetic - Ventral Vagal)
- Out-of-Alignment Fight/Flight States (Sympathetic)
- & the Out-of-Alignment Freeze State
  (Parasympathetic - Dorsal Vagal)

There is a structure or hierarchy of how these form and how we move within our Nervous System States. Think of them like building/stacking blocks

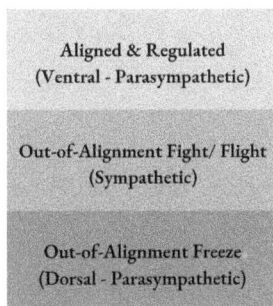

Aligned & Regulated
(Ventral - Parasympathetic)

Out-of-Alignment Fight/ Flight
(Sympathetic)

Out-of-Alignment Freeze
(Dorsal - Parasympathetic)

..................................

Our Neuroception is often what causes the blockages we have in our Manifesting ability. For example, think about what Amanda Frances calls energetic setpoints; "the amount of money you can't imagine earning more than." You often hear people saying that they want to make six figures each month in their business... however for whatever reason, when they think about earning the six-figure month, they start to feel anxious and worried, their heart rate goes up, and they begin to doubt themselves... All of these internal changes and reactions to thinking about making six figures each month are picked up by their Neuroception Processes.

This then sends warning bells to their brain saying that earning six figures is dangerous. As a result, this can pull them Out-of-Alignment with that goal. It's like they could mentally imagine it but their Nervous Systems could not imagine making six figures each month because it feels too dangerous.

This is where being curious about and working through your limiting beliefs comes into play. This is also where visualising, feeling the emotions as if it has already happened, Vagus Nerve exercises, affirmations, and shifting your energy and expectations help to rewire this belief. If your Nervous System can't imagine earning six figures, choose an income goal where your Nervous System feels safe for that to happen... Make it realistic for your Nervous System. Once you meet that income level, you can change your energetic setpoint to a higher amount.

For example when I initially started one of my businesses in 2018, mentally I had a goal to have a million-dollar year. However realistically, my Nervous System could not imagine that at all. A million dollars in profit, an infant, no external help, a partner that worked away a lot, and a brand new business. My Nervous system was in stitches... No way was that achievable to it. There were too many internal Danger Signs happening. So I held on to the dream that I would one day have a million-dollar year and at the same time I set a realistic and safer goal for myself. I made my energetic set point to have a $5,000 year and did a lot of mindset and Nervous System work around making $5,000 before my daughter turned one. That decision felt far safer to my Nervous System.

# HOMEWORK

...............................

It's time to create a list of your Neuroception Danger and Safety Signs. In doing so, we can identify things, experiences, and interactions that help our Nervous Systems feel safe, connected, and present as well as all the things that work against our Nervous System.

Identifying our Safety Signs enables us to become aware of and use them to calm our Nervous System when we experience a form of stress and help us return to a holistically Aligned & Regulated (Ventral) State. Identifying our Danger Signs can help us to look at ways we can possibly reduce or remove these in our daily lives so that we experience more time in a Flow state.

Each person will have their own unique list of Safety and Danger signs. However, I have included an example list of Safety and Danger signs for you to refer back to when or if needed. Your Safety and Danger Signs can be made up of people, things, scents, textures, foods, drinks, environments, money goals, animals, weather patterns, certain topics, activities, clothing/outfits, modes of transport etc.

# EXAMPLES OF SAFETY SIGNS

...........................................

- alone time
- coffee or hot beverages
- being in nature
- certain songs
- certain scents
- showers
- cool morning breeze
- comfortable cosy clothes
- being in bed
- fresh sheets
- clean surfaces & house
- meditation
- smiles
- quiet environments
- certain tv shows
- baths
- certain selfcare rituals
- coffee with friends
- organised house
- structure & routine
- healthy family
- cuddles
- weekends
- sleep ins
- spa days

- pet cuddles
- walks
- the ocean/beach/river
- basking in sunlight
- watching the sun set
- stargazing
- favourite food
- certain season/time of day
- chats with friends
- exercise
- getting hair/nails done
- listening to podcast
- certain colours
- fresh flowers
- ice cold water
- clean car
- holidays
- supportive partner
- being heard/seen/validated
- intimacy with partner
- home décor items
- bees/butterflies in garden
- rain

- massages
- therapist
- heat packs
- spiritual advisor
- reading
- mindful activities
- getting off work
- partner gets home
- full nights sleep
- weekends
- deep breathing
- brunch
- social media break
- plants
- certain income levels
- driving at night
- oracle cards
- smudging
- journaling

# My Safety Signs

List of things, people, song or situations etc. that make me feel safe:

| | | |
|---|---|---|
| _____ | _____ | _____ |
| _____ | _____ | _____ |
| _____ | _____ | _____ |
| _____ | _____ | _____ |
| _____ | _____ | _____ |
| _____ | _____ | _____ |
| _____ | _____ | _____ |
| _____ | _____ | _____ |
| _____ | _____ | _____ |
| _____ | _____ | _____ |
| _____ | _____ | _____ |
| _____ | _____ | _____ |
| _____ | _____ | _____ |

Reflective questions:

- How could I add more of these to my everyday routines? (spending more time in nature, diffusing certain scents, investing in new bed linen, making mindful routines around my night-time routine or morning coffee?)

- What Safety Signs could I use or visualise when I experience stress? (visualise the ocean, using an essential oil/perfume, changing into comfortable clothes, playing certain songs, calling a safety sign person, and cuddling kids or pet?)

# EXAMPLES OF DANGER SIGNS

....................................

- raised voices
- loud noises
- being rushed
- clutter
- social media
- certain income levels
- bickering
- feeling powerless
- plans changing
- crowds
- getting out the door
- grocery shopping
- sickness
- sick children
- bills
- filling car up with petrol/gas
- food types or allergies
- going out in public with kids
- certain animals
- being in public
- the dark
- empty car lots
- walking with headphones

- having a low bank balance
- goal setting
- parents/ in-laws
- unsupportive partner
- partner working away/nightshift
- making meals/snacks
- watching the news
- being ignored
- intimacy with partner
- rainy days
- driving
- meal planning
- mental load or household
- chores
- feeling stuck
- feeling alone
- feeling judged
- feeling not good enough
- noisy kid's toys
- laundry piles
- home safety
- home's location
- job or partner's job
- catching public transport

# My Danger Signs

List of things, people, song or situations etc. that make me feel unsafe:

| | | |
|---|---|---|
| _____ | _____ | _____ |
| _____ | _____ | _____ |
| _____ | _____ | _____ |
| _____ | _____ | _____ |
| _____ | _____ | _____ |
| _____ | _____ | _____ |
| _____ | _____ | _____ |
| _____ | _____ | _____ |
| _____ | _____ | _____ |
| _____ | _____ | _____ |
| _____ | _____ | _____ |
| _____ | _____ | _____ |
| _____ | _____ | _____ |
| _____ | _____ | _____ |

Reflective questions:

- How could I remove or reduce more of these from my everyday routines? (social media break, click and collect groceries, pack bags and/or lunch the night before, declutter, set and hold boundaries, shop early in the morning/on weekdays to avoid crowds, hire support for a short while, focus more on creating a calming and safe home environment, or investing in additional security measures etc.)

# THREE

....................................

# RECAP

I thought that it would be a good idea to stop here and recap on everything covered so far. It's a lot to take in, isn't it?

**Key take-aways so far:**

- We have 4 main Nervous States we move between each day:
  Alignment
  **Regulation** *(Calming Ventral Vagal - Front of Vagus Nerve)*

  Out-of-Alignment & Dysregulation
  **Fight** *(Sympathetic - Mobilising Energy)*
  **Flight** *(Sympathetic - Mobilising Energy)*
  **Freeze** *(Immobilising Dorsal Vagal - Parasympathetic - Back of Vagus Nerve)*


- Our Nervous System and its states have a direct influence on our Manifesting abilities. It can pull us in and out of Alignment/Regulation automatically. It also has a direct influence on our energetic state and magnetism.


- Our Nervous System and Neuroceptive Processes often cause blockages in our manifesting abilities because there is a mismatch between our abundance mindset and how safe our Nervous System feels with that goal or desire. It can also be what is unconsciously attracting low-vibrational things into our lives. A lot of people and gurus are unaware of or don't take the time to explain/ regulate their Nervous System's to holistically align with what they want to manifest. They tend to focus on mindset "Level One and Up" topics without building a strong Regulated foundation.

- In order to match with our mindset, manifestations, wants and desires, we need to be holistically aligned. The missing key is regulating our Nervous System and using the calming Parasympathetic energy of the Vagus Nerve.

- Just like Abraham Hicks mentions, we can't stay within the 'Vortex' - or in Alignment - all day. We move throughout the different Nervous System States (Both Regulation and Stress Responses) depending on situations that arise.

- Having a healthier and optimally functioning Vagus Nerve can help move us back into the 'Vortex' easier and quicker after we experience stress.

- Our Neuroception is constantly searching for Signs of Safety and Danger within our environment and desires. It does this by searching for instinctive cues, internal or external cues, and cues determined by all of our life and ancestors' life experiences via Epigenetics (the modification of gene expression within our DNA.)

- Our Nervous System sort of acts like a balance scale. If our Autonomic Nervous System determines, via Neuroception, that there are more signs of Safety than Danger we remain in our high-frequency, Aligned, Regulated State (Ventral). If there are more Danger Signs we get pushed Out-of-Alignment into our Fight/Flight/Freeze low-vibration stress responses automatically.

- We can recalibrate our Safety and Danger signs, as well as our thoughts, beliefs emotional reactions, behaviours etc. thanks to Neuroplasticity.

- Each Nervous System state have their specific purposes in life however, the low-frequency Survival Stress Responses are not the space you want to be living in let alone manifesting from. This can be the cause of all the hit and miss manifestations that have been occurring.

In the next few chapters we are going to explore each of the four main Nervous System states and how they influence the stories we tell ourselves as well as our thoughts, actions, emotions, values, and manifesting abilities.

Autonomic
Nervous System

Sympathetic Branch
Out of Alignment
(Fight & Flight)

Parasympathetic
Branch

Ventral Vagal
Branch
Aligned & Flow
(Regulated)
(Front of our Vagus
Nerve)

Dorsal Vagal
Branch
Out of Alignment
(Freeze)
(Back of our Vagus
Nerve)

There is no fixed physical reality, no single perception of the world, just numerous ways of interpreting world views as dictated by one's Nervous System and the specific environment of our planetary existence.

—

DEEPAK CHOPRA

# FOUR

......................................

# -ALIGNMENT-
## OUR REGULATED
## NERVOUS SYSTEM STATE

The top section of our Nervous System States building block metaphor is our Aligned Regulated State (Ventral - Parasympathetic). It is our flow, social engagement and connection state. If we have a well-functioning Nervous System, this is the predominant state we find ourselves in - holistically in Alignment.

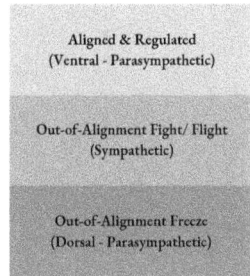

Aligned & Regulated (Ventral - Parasympathetic)

Out-of-Alignment Fight/ Flight (Sympathetic)

Out-of-Alignment Freeze (Dorsal - Parasympathetic)

In this state, our Neuroception has detected more Safety Signs than Danger Signs and has determined that who we are with, the environment we are in, or the situation we find ourselves in is safe for our physical bodies.

When we are in our Aligned Regulated (Ventral) state we:

- are present in the moment and show pro-social behaviours
- capable of entering a flow state and taking aligned and inspired action
- in a better position to manifest as we are holistically aligned
- are capable of a "connected" interaction with another human being
- vibrating at a higher frequency
- can rest, relax, and meditate
- walk around feeling unafraid, enjoying our day, eating with friends and family
- feel safe, calm, happy, creative, curious, playful
- we can identify and manage/work through some tolerable stress without getting overwhelmed

This Aligned Regulated (Ventral) state supports us in the feeling of being physically safe, experiencing flow, and being able to emotionally connect to others. In this Regulated Aligned State, at some level, our Nervous System believes we are safe.

Abraham Hicks makes reference to being in an Aligned Regulated State as being "tuned in, tapped in, turned on." All of which occurs when we are emotionally regulated.

# FIVE

...............................

# -OUT OF ALIGNMENT-
## OUR DYSREGULATED
## NERVOUS SYSTEM STATES

The middle section of our Nervous System States are our Out-of-Alignment Fight/Flight States (Sympathetic). These are our mobilising energy response and our immediate stress reaction. Once our Neuroception determines that there are more Danger Signs than Safety, we are automatically pushed into either a Fight or Flight

> Aligned & Regulated
> (Ventral - Parasympathetic)
>
> Out-of-Alignment Fight/ Flight
> (Sympathetic)
>
> Out-of-Alignment Freeze
> (Dorsal - Parasympathetic)

survival response and these responses affect nearly every organ in our body. It responds to the Neuroception Danger Signs by bringing a quick burst of energy (cortisol and adrenaline) to mobilise us with the energy needed to either fight and/or flee what our Nervous System perceives to be a threat.

As we go through our day we dip in and out of this Fight/Flight state. The Fight/Flight survival state isn't always a bad thing and comes in handy in certain situations when we need a burst of mobilising energy like when we find ourselves:

- slamming on our car's brakes
- jumping out of the way of a falling object like a saucepan lid
- ducking when a ball or bird comes flying at us
- getting quick bursts of energy during exercise or amorous activities etc.

When we are in our Fight/Flight (Sympathetic) state we:

- may feel angry, on edge, hyper-aroused or anxious
- may get sensory overload

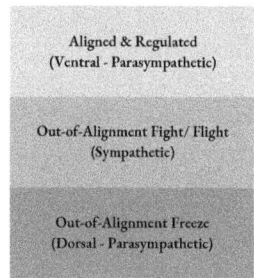

- aren't capable of entering a Flow state and often find taking aligned or inspired action frustrating and unachievable or confusing
- we aren't holistically aligned to manifest in a way we want to
- we end up being in a low-frequency/vibrational space and in turn start to attract low-frequency/vibrational things
- find that little things may set us off easily or feel touched out
- may raise our voice, our muscles tense up, and our breathing rate increases
- we may even feel the need to escape/take a break from the current situation.

Now, this Fight/Flight stress response is only really meant to be in the immediate stage of dealing with something stressful- 10-15 minutes tops. That would give us enough energy and time to Fight off or Flee the danger (or Sabre Tooth Tiger back in the day). Ideally, we would then recover from the surge of mobilising energy, after fighting off or fleeing from the danger. In Fight or Flight, at some level, our Nervous System believes we can still survive whatever threat it thinks is dangerous.

.....................................

The bottom section of our Nervous System States is our Out-of-Alignment Freeze State (Dorsal - Parasympathetic). It's the opposite of our Fight/Flight (Sympathetic) Nervous System's mobilising response. It is our immobilising energy response and our secondary reaction to stress. This is a survival, self-preservation, energy-conserving response that makes death less likely if we are attacked and injured. An example of this in nature is when a gazelle instantly goes limp/plays dead until the threat passes or the lion lets go it then immediately gets up and runs away from the lion.

In this Freeze State, our Neuroception has detected significant amounts of Danger Signs and our Nervous System determines that we can't or can no longer Fight or Flee from the perceived threat, that we are trapped, and that there is now a life-threatening risk to us.

It responds to the Neuroception Danger Signs by going into self-preservation mode. It slows down our bodily functions to focus on keeping our emergency life support systems running. As we go through our day we may dip in and out of this Freeze State. Like Fight/Flight, our Freeze Survival State isn't always a bad thing. We use some of the Freeze immobilising energy when we meditate or rest.

When we are in our Freeze (Dorsal - Parasympathetic) state we may:
- feel burnt out, experience chronic fatigue, depressive moods
- feel hopeless
- have digestive issues due to our body slowing down to support our emergency life support systems
- aren't capable of entering a flow state and can't comprehend taking any sort of aligned or inspired action
- we aren't holistically aligned at all to manifest in a way we want to
- we end up being in a very low-frequency/vibrational space and in-turn start to attract very low-frequency/vibrational things
- feel so heavy and sluggish
- experience difficulty in communicating with others
- brain fog and memory problems
- find it hard to communicate or accesses our emotions
- feel like we are just going through the motions
- feel very lightheaded or dizzy and can even dissociate or pass out

In our Freeze state, our Nervous System is trying its hardest to help us survive the perceived or real life-threatening danger so that we can either Fight or Flee from it again. It tries to keep us alive by slowing us down and keeping our bodies as still as possible. A lot of people, the majority being entrepreneurial and hustle culture minded people, end up living in this state as they unconsciously push themselves so much so that their Nervous System becomes severely Dysregulated.

# HOMEWORK

....................................

In this section, we will create a personalised Nervous System Blueprint to identify key emotions, behaviours, values, actions, and beliefs you experience in each of the Nervous System states you move through each day. It will also show you how your Nervous State influences your mindset, energetic frequency, and manifesting abilities.

When working your way though this activity, try to determine what your baseline Nervous System State is.

- What State do you currently resonate with? Aligned/Fight/Flight/Freeze?
- Which state do you think you are living in and manifesting from?
- Are you mainly Regulated and dipping in and out of Fight/Flight?
- Are you mainly living in Fight/Flight and dipping in and out of Freeze?
- Are you mainly living in Freeze?

This work is inspired by the research of Deb Dana. I have included an example for you to refer back to when or if needed.

# Alignment

## Regulated Ventral Blueprint:

### When I am holistically aligned

**I am:**

calm, inspired, happy, optimistic, organised, emotionally and mentally flexible, and relaxed for the most part- there are little bits of stress here and there but it doesn't affect me too much

**My body Feels:**

relaxed, balanced, grounded, centred, light, relaxed shoulders, unclenched jaw, flexible, strong, electric, energised, healthy

**Manifestation & taking aligned action feels:**

exciting, natural, easy, joyful, like it just makes sense to do, expansive, thrilling, amazing, an urge or feels like I am being drawn to it, simple, things keep aligning and coming into my path without resistance, it's like taking easy steps, synchronicities and signs keep appearing, wealth and abundance pouring in

**I have the urge to:**

create, take aligned action, follow my intuition, go deep into learning and work that lights me up, play, socialise, participate in mindful activities, meditate, connect with my family, rest and relax

When I am holistically aligned I am:

_____

_____

_____

_____

_____

_____

My body Feels:

_____

_____

_____

_____

_____

Manifestation & taking aligned action feels:

_____

_____

_____

_____

_____

I have the urge to:

_____

_____

_____

_____

_____

Other things to note:

How does being in this Flow state affect my sleep? eating patterns? energy levels, relationships with my partner/family/friends, how does it affect my day to day life?

_____

_____

_____

_____

_____

_____

_____

_____

_____

_____

_____

_____

_____

_____

_____

_____

_____

_____

_____

_____

_____

_____

# Out-of-Alignment

## Fight Response Blueprint:

| |
|---|
| Aligned & Regulated (Ventral - Parasympathetic) |
| Out-of-Alignment Fight/ Flight (Sympathetic) |
| Out-of-Alignment Freeze (Dorsal - Parasympathetic) |

## When I am in my Out-of-Alignment Fight Stress response

**I am:**

stressed, overwhelmed, angry, frustrated, on edge, overstimulated, my brain is scattered, and everything feels like it's setting me off, jealous, annoyed by others, not following my intuition and path

**My body Feels:**

off balance, blocked, tense & tight - my muscles especially: clenched hands, arms, raised tight shoulders, clenched jaw. My muscle ache from being tense all the time, and low vibrational

**Manifestation & taking aligned action feels:**

hard, annoying, and irritating, like I am meeting challenges and resistance every step I take, I am attracting more unexpected bills and problems, confusing, and taking on other people's energy and ideas that don't align with my path

**I have the urge to:**

yell, scream, shout or raise my voice, start over, buy or enrol in other people's courses hoping they have the answers - in turn get angry at myself or other because it didn't work, take any action even if it goes against my intuition

When I am in my Out-of-Alignment Fight State I am:

_____
_____
_____
_____
_____
_____

My body Feels:

_____
_____
_____
_____
_____

Manifestation & taking aligned action feels:

_____
_____
_____
_____
_____

I have the urge to:

_____
_____
_____
_____
_____

Other things to note:

How does being in this Fight state affect my sleep? eating patterns? energy levels, relationships with my partner/family/friends, how does it affect my day to day life?

---
---
---
---
---
---
---
---
---
---
---
---
---
---
---
---
---
---
---
---
---
---
---
---
---
---
---

# Out-of-Alignment

## Flight Response Blueprint:

## When I am in my Out-of-Alignment Flight Stress response

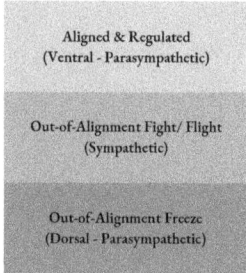

**I am:**

anxious, on edge, constantly doing unnecessary things, feel tired but wired at the same time, anxious or afraid

**My body Feels:**

off balance, blocked, touched out and overstimulated, it feels a bit off - especially my stomach, I get an anxious, sweaty palms, racing thoughts, my body feels like it needs to move and not rest

**Manifestation & taking aligned action feels:**

too hard and too much but at the same time I feel like doing every little tip and trick to try and get some sort of flow state happening, manic manifestation, taking on other people energy and ideas that don't align with my path

**I have the urge to:**

get away – escape my house, my family, and responsibilities. Stop focusing on anything spiritual, give up, I need alone time. I have the urge to just do things to help me feel in some sort of control even if they don't align with my path, procrastinate, try every tip and trick all at once - overload

When I am in my Out-of-Alignment Flight State I am:

_____

_____

_____

_____

_____

_____

My body Feels:

_____

_____

_____

_____

_____

Manifestation & taking aligned action feels:

_____

_____

_____

_____

_____

I have the urge to:

_____

_____

_____

_____

_____

Other things to note:

How does being in this Flight state affect my sleep? eating patterns? energy levels, relationships with my partner/family/friends, how does it affect my day to day life?

_____

_____

_____

_____

_____

_____

_____

_____

_____

_____

_____

_____

_____

_____

_____

_____

_____

_____

_____

_____

_____

_____

_____

# Out-of-Alignment

## Freeze Response Blueprint:

## When I am in my Out-of-Alignment Freeze Stress response

**I am:**

drowning and struggling to make it through the days. I feel numb, lost, in a daze. I hate this I don't know how much longer I am going to last at this rate. I am burnt out. I can't remember or find anything

**My body Feels:**

severely off balance, blocked, exhausted, chronically fatigued, pain everywhere that seems to move places, weak and heavy, sluggish, spacey and disconnected. I have digestive problems

**Manifestation & taking aligned action feels:**

hopeless, unrealistic, out of reach, just a fantasy that feels unattainable, too hard to even being figuring out what I need to do

**I have the urge to:**

spend all day - every day in bed, sleep, pause time/life, just stop, give up

When I am in my Out-of-Alignment Freeze State I am:

_____

_____

_____

_____

_____

_____

My body Feels:

_____

_____

_____

_____

_____

Manifestation & taking aligned action feels:

_____

_____

_____

_____

_____

I have the urge to:

_____

_____

_____

_____

_____

Other things to note:

How does being in this Freeze state affect my sleep? eating patterns? energy levels, relationships with my partner/family/friends, how does it affect my day to day life?

_____

_____

_____

_____

_____

_____

_____

_____

_____

_____

_____

_____

_____

_____

_____

_____

_____

_____

_____

_____

_____

_____

Our Reticular Activating System is like an intention-setting machine.

———

EVA HATTIN

# SIX

......................................

# 'LUCKY GIRL SYNDROME'

Have you ever wondered how some people seem to have so much luck and abundance? It may have to do with their Reticular Activating System. The Reticular Activating System (RAS) is a network of neurons located in our brain stem that filters out unnecessary information. Its main job is to figure out what our brain needs to focus on during the day then looks for confirmation of those things.

Each day our RAS sorts through the millions of bits of information & stimuli that come into our brain each moment. With all the information coming in, our RAS can roughly process about 26 pieces of information at any given moment. The rest of the stimuli then gets filtered out.

It's kind of like an intention-setting machine. When we decide our intention and desires, each day we wake up our RAS searches for things that affirm and promote them. However, our mental and Nervous System State plays a huge role in how we perceive our world and influences our RAS (think back to the last chapter's homework where we mapped out your Nervous System Blueprint). **This is why being in a holistically aligned and regulated state is so important. If we wake up in a Fight/Flight/Freeze/Closed-Minded State...**

*"I feel like shit; Nothing is going right; My manifestations are unattainable etc..."*
We can unconsciously set our RAS intention to be on the lookout for things to confirm this and filter out anything that goes against this.

**If we wake up in an Aligned, Open-Minded State...**

*"I am so truly abundant; I am a money magnet; I am calm and relaxed etc..."*

We are setting our RAS intention to seek out things to confirm this and our success.

Over time this process gets easier. It becomes automatic as we set and confirm these new thought/belief patterns. The more we are in a Regulated Nervous System State and focus on our desires/manifestations, the more we invite and energetically align them into our lives as our RAS is now primed for abundance. We also end up easily aligning ourselves and spotting ways to take inspired action towards our manifestations and desires.

Our RAS is also stimulated when we practise affirmations and set goals for ourselves. When we set SMARt goals (Specific, Measurable, Achievable, Realistic, *timebound - I don't really subscribe to being bound by time especially when manifesting*) we are priming our brains to look for opportunities and resources that can assist us in meeting those goals. When that happens so many synchronicities and pathways appear before us that makes taking aligned and inspired action easy and natural.

# SEVEN

......................................

# HOW WE BECOME OUT-OF-ALIGNMENT

Out-of-Alignment is not a fun place to be in nor is it a desirable place to manifest from. Nobody wants to be constantly attracting low-vibrational things and people. There are numerous ways we can end up Out-of-Alignment and living in our Dysregulated Survival Stress Response states of Fight, Flight, and Freeze. There are physiological and emotional reasons, reasons associated with our home or work environment, reasons stemming from our limiting beliefs, and/or energetic and spiritual reasons etc.

In this next section, I am going to walk you through some of the main reasons we may find ourselves being automatically pushed into or living in a dysregulated state. Afterwards we will explore strategies to help move us back into alignment as well as ways to get out of living predominately in a low-frequency stress state. This will then help to prime our Reticular Activating System and begin to energetically attract and align with abundance.

# WINDOW OF TOLERANCE

..................................

We all have a thing called a Window of Tolerance, which comes from the work of Dan Seigel. You can think of our Window of Tolerance as our Nervous System's Safe Space.

Our Window of Tolerance describes our optimal zone of how much stress we can endure while managing our emotions and going about our daily lives before we are pushed over our limit and into our Out-of-Alignment Survival Stress States of Fight/Flight/Freeze.

In a perfect world, we would all have big beautiful Windows of Tolerance. We would be able to remain in an optimal holistic Flow state and hardly get pushed over our Nervous System's limits and into our Dysregulated Survival States (Fight/Flight/Freeze).

But because the world isn't perfect and we are only humans, some of us have developed a narrower Window of Tolerance - meaning what we can tolerate is a lot smaller before we are pushed over our limits and into Survival Stress Responses.

When our brain or Nervous System senses a stressor, or even the possibility of one, people who have narrower Windows of Tolerance can enter into an Unaligned Dysregulated State (Fight/Flight/Freeze) quicker than others who have bigger Windows facing the same stressors.

People with narrower Windows of Tolerance can end up hanging out in and living in their low-frequency stress states (predominantly living in Fight, Flight or Freeze), hardly ever making it back into their Windows of Tolerance or high-frequency, Aligned, and Regulated (Ventral) state. 3

Being within our Window of Tolerance doesn't mean we are calm all the time & don't experience stress. It means that we are able to work through stressful situations and emotions while still being in the Regulated (Ventral) state.

Being within our Window of Tolerance means we are still in our high-frequency state while moving through and handling stress as it comes up. Just like Abraham Hicks says we can't constantly remain the Vortex, it's also not possible to remain in our Aligned, Regulated Window of Tolerance all the time. However, it is possible to gradually widen our Window of Tolerance so we spend less time emotionally dysregulated and more time holistically aligned.

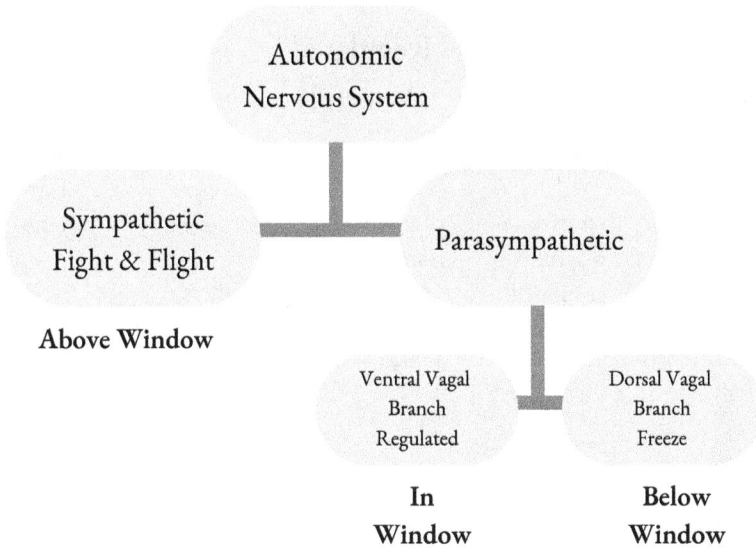

Autonomic
Nervous System

Sympathetic
Fight & Flight

Parasympathetic

**Above Window**

Ventral Vagal
Branch
Regulated

Dorsal Vagal
Branch
Freeze

**In
Window**

**Below
Window**

# Hyper-arousal
# Fight/Flight
# (Sympathetic)

**Above Your Window**

Low Frequency

| | | | |
|---|---|---|---|
| scared | avoiding | aggression | overwhelmed |
| anxious | escaping | irritated | defensive |
| frantic | enraged | frustrated | restless |
| nervous | hypervigilant | impulsive | irritated |
| panicked | rigid | yelling | |

# Regulated
# (Ventral)

**In Your Window of Tolerance**

High Frequency

safe      centred
open      reflective

| | | | |
|---|---|---|---|
| happy | creative | empathetic & | curious   switched on |
| joyful | playful | compassionate | |
| energised | grounded | able to connect with others | |
| rest | mindful | ability to handle challenges & stressful situations | |
| | calm | ability to work through emotions | |

Low Frequency

| | | | |
|---|---|---|---|
| lethargic | frozen | detached | low motivation |
| numb | confused | disassociated | withdrawn |
| depressive | lost | trance like | derealisation |
| checked out | brain fog | feeling helpless | memory fog |
| | | feeling hopeless | little emotion |
| | | | trapped |

**Below Your Window**

# Hypo-arousal
# Freeze
(Dorsal Parasympathetic)

Windows of Tolerance can be vastly different from person to person. How wide your Window is can depend on several factors. It can also change day by day and throughout the day depending on the environment and the situations you find yourself in.

Some common factors that affect Windows of Tolerance include:

- Your Mum/birth mother's stress levels in her pregnancy - The state of her Nervous system during pregnancy determines your baseline state. If she was severely stressed - you come out thinking that stress is normal.
- Your birth & childhood experiences
- Your parent/caregiver's parenting style & emotional intelligence
- Not having your needs met growing up
- Lack of support from partner, family, and friends
- Your physical environment growing up and the one you're in now
- Your ability to self-regulate emotions/ emotional intelligence
- Any traumatic experiences (both big trauma & little trauma)
- An existing mental health and/or health conditions
- Illness, chronic stress
- Discrimination and racism
- Lack of societal emotional intelligence/literacy
- Working or living in high-stress environments
- Fast-paced society
- Sleep deprivation
- Separation from family, partner, loved ones, your baby/child
- Taking on the mental load
- Criticism, overwhelming advice, unwanted advice, conflicting advice
- Excessive noise or other sensory stimuli
- Extra clutter in household
- Stressful personal and global events
- Pushing yourself & burnout
- Spiritual & Energetic causes - see future sections

# ALLOSTATIC LOAD

..................................

Abundance is our birth right. We all deserve the very best in all areas of our lives but sometimes this appears to not be the case. Building up an Allostatic load may be the reason behind this.

Our Nervous System can start to adapt to stress & our stress hormones causing our baseline Nervous System state to be a Survival Stress Response instead of being Aligned Regulation. We can adapt to living in a low-vibrational state.

This can happen if we have been:

- experiencing chronic stress
- have developed an unhealthy Vagus Nerve that is not functioning optimally (Low Vagal Tone- explained more in a few pages),
- have been living outside of our Window of Tolerance & in our Out-of-Alignment Survival States for a long period of time (Fight/Flight/Freeze)

As our bodies adapt to our stress hormones, it causes us to change our baseline Nervous System State from being predominantly Aligned Regulation (Ventral) to a Survival Stress Response (Fight/Flight/Freeze). This is called Allostasis, (Homeostasis being Regulation (Ventral).

In other words, our new everyday Nervous System State = stress. Cool, but it gets better... When we do dip back into Regulation, our Neuroception sends a message to the brain that this calm and relaxed state is a potential threat as it is different to our new Baseline Fight/Flight/Freeze State or stress. Exactly what we want right?! No!

Over time we can also build up an Allostatic Load which is the cumulative effect of the wear and tear on the body and Nervous System from being in this heightened stress response state for a prolonged time. Remember, the

Fight/Flight/Freeze response was only ever meant to happen for 10-15 minutes tops - just enough time to fight or flee a threat. It was never designed to be a state that you lived in. Think of all the damage that can come from living in a state where you are constantly flooded with stress hormones. The Wear and Tear that can come from living in a Survival Stress Response can be anything from a reduced immune system, digestive issues, inflammation and cardiovascular issues to pregnancy, cognitive, emotional and mental health issues. Anything and everything really as our Autonomic Nervous System influences and is connected to all our major organs and processes. This stress has an enormous impact on our manifesting abilities and magnitism

To reduce our Allostatic Load and move back to Regulation being our baseline state, we need to look at both our behavioural and environmental structures. We need to make sure that most of our basic needs are getting met every day, we are adding more Safety Signs to our lives, reducing or removing as many of our Danger Signs, and working on strengthening our Vagus Nerve.

Over time, we will start to move into and hang out in our Window of Tolerance more often and be able to use specific strategies to help us self-regulate. Now that seems like a lot to do considering those who have developed an Allostatic Load are most likely severely burnt out. I admit when I began the journey of recalibrating my Nervous System it seemed impossible - hello Freeze State Mindset. However, the easy Vagus Nerve exercises, rituals, and activities found towards the end of this book made returning my baseline Nervous System State easier than I thought. In saying that, it wasn't a quick process. There aren't any shortcuts to healing. For those who are like me or are interested, I have included my self-care implementation stages plan for you to follow. This was the exact plan I took to help me move back into regulation.

In the next section we will explore and determine how healthy our Vagus Nerves are.

# VAGAL TONE

·····························

Let's think back to our time in the womb and our birth for a second. When we were born, we have something called low Myelination - *Myelin: the protective sheath or layer around our nerves that acts as an insulator; helping all the electrical signals in our nerves get to their intended destination*

As infants, the protective Myelin layer around our Vagus Nerve is weak. If our development isn't interrupted by the age of three, a healthy protective Myelin layer is formed around our nerves. If our parents were nurturing, safe and calm caregivers - the healthier our protective Myelin layer would be as our mirror neurons detected and replicated that Regulated (Ventral) state they showed us by nurturing and co-regulating us. As we age, all our life experiences then add to this and influence how strong and healthy our Vagus Nerve are Myelin sheath are.

When our Vagus Nerve is healthy and functioning well it is referred to as having a "High Vagal Tone." Having a high/strong Vagal Tone means we can return to a calm and happy Regulated Flow (Ventral) state quickly after a stressful situation as it has an optimal Myelin Sheath.

When our Vagus Nerve isn't functioning optimally, it's known as having a "Low Vagal Tone." Low vagal tone is caused by having weak or deteriorated Myelin sheath causing the electrical signals to be sent at a much slower pace. Living under chronic stress or in Fight/Flight survival mode can weaken the strength of our Vagus Nerve - the wear and tear that comes from building up an Allostatic Load.

Having a Low Vagal Tone means it can take our bodies longer to recover from stressful situations and is associated with many health conditions and can lead to a multitude of symptoms and health problems as the Vagus Nerve is connected to all of our main organs and bodily functions. For those who have a Low Vagal Tone, it may feel like they are stuck in a heightened stress survival state (Fight/Flight/Freeze) or stuck in a low-frequency state.

Vagal Nerve Stimulation is one way we can improve our Vagal Tone. You can have this done invasively via your health practitioner and/or via non-invasive strategies - some of which can be found in the future chapters.

As this is an emerging field, not a whole lot of research has been done as of yet. However, there has been some research done so far that has shown promising evidence that the strategies and nutritional information, found in the future sections, improve Vagal Function.

There also may be other underlying/root causes that can cause someone to have a Low Vagal tone (Trauma/Neglect/Illness etc.) so speaking with your Doctor/s about your symptoms is the first point of call in your healing journey.-

.................................

A non-exhaustive list of symptoms associated with having a Low Vagal Tone

- Anxious or Depressive feelings or mood
- Highly stressed or overwhelmed
- Poor concentration and attention span
- Migraines and headaches
- Chronic fatigue
- Weight problems
- Lack of motivation and desire
- Quick to emotionally dysregulate -snap
- Digestive problems – constipation, diarrhoea, gas and bloating, nausea, IBS, reflux, leaky gut, food intolerance or sensitivities, poor digestion
- Problems with food textures or is a picky eater
- High or low gag response

- Tripping over things/ balance is off
- Poor posture – hunched over/ slouched
- You feel uncomfortable in your body
- Muscle tension and pain
- Inflammation in body
- Low energy, Feeling Sluggish
- Slow/Hard to get moving
- Feet and legs feel heavy
- Need more alone time to rest and reset, especially after socialising
- Finds it difficult to socialise
- Feel like you are just going through the motions
- Struggle to fall asleep initially and after waking at night
- Wake frequently in the night
- Needing the perfect conditions to fall asleep
- Waking up at every sound
- Snoring or Mouth breathing
- Trouble reaching your tongue to the roof of your mouth

Vagal Tone Exercise:

Check to see if your uvula deviates or pulls to the left or the right (instead of rising) when you perform an "ah, ah, ah" sound with an open mouth. Use a tongue depressor, and flashlight, and have a partner check your uvula as you perform the sound. If it doesn't rise, it can be a symptom of having a Low Vagal Tone.

Remember that the Vagus Nerve is the key to help us move back into Alignment which means ideally we want an optimally functioning, healthy Vagus Nerve with high Myelination so that we can move back into alignment and regulation quicker and easier after we experience stress.

"Care for your psyche...
know thyself, for once
we know ourselves, we
may learn how to care
for ourselves."

———

SOCRATES

# EIGHT

......................................

# HUMAN DESIGN & OUR NERVOUS SYSTEM

Okay... time for some spiritual reasons why we can get pulled Out-of-Alignment. The first one being not living according to your Human Design. For those who aren't familiar, Human Design is a complex and nuanced system created by Ra Uru Hu based on ancient and modern spiritual systems like I Ching, Astrology etc. It uses your exact time, date, and place of birth, much like how Astrology uses Natal charts, to map out your unique personality and provides a sort of manual or guide to living in a manner that is aligned with your unique design or blueprint. **Now if this isn't your thing, feel free to skip this section!**

To find your Human Design, and then apply it to the following information, you will need to generate a personal Human Design Chart.

This can be done via a variety of websites, some free to download & others where you can pay to get a more in-depth report from a HD expert.

For free design charts, see the following business:

- Jovian Archive
  https://www.jovianarchive.com/get_your_chart

- My Human Design by Jenna Zoe -
  https://www.myhumandesign.com/get-your-chart/

- My Bodygraph
  https://www.mybodygraph.com/free-bodygraph

If you are new to Human Design, I would advise you to take some time to explore and apply strategies and concepts to your Design. In Human Design (as well as Gene Keys) there is quite a bit to unpack initially. Once you have spent some time experimenting and learning about your Human Design, you can come back to this chapter and apply the following information to your Design.

To begin with, I spent some time researching and learning about My Design, I then bought a few different in-depth reports and online courses to help me unpack and understand myself more. As my Human Design Experiment progressed, I began to see ways we can use Human Design to influence our emotional regulation and flow state. If we aren't following our Human Design, we tend to push ourselves our of our Window of Tolerance more frequently and work against our natural state of being.

# THE FOUR ARROWS

·······································

The 4 Arrows otherwise known as Variables or The Four Transformations traditionally show us our cognitive designs; how we experience life, how we are designed to approach our environments and routines, how we are designed to manifest and how we are designed to take in information. I have explored and experimented with how these variables align with emotional intelligence and how we can best approach regulating and nurturing our Nervous Systems for abundance. I am going to focus solely on the Digestion Variable & then explore the different Environments found in Human Design.

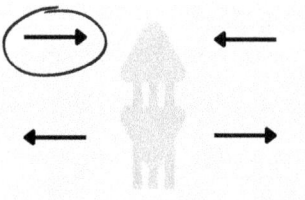

# Digestion: Top Left Arrow

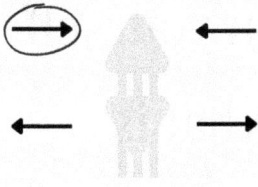

This is the arrow that explains the circumstances needed to thrive and our Nervous Systems to feel safe enough to be in our Aligned, Regulated State. This part of our chart can tell us about how we best digest (take in) both food and information from our environment. It also gives some insight as to whether routines and structure will work with our design. This can be especially important when creating an environment that nurtures our Nervous Systems to feel safe and in an Aligned Flow state.

**Right Facing:**

If your Digestion arrow is right facing, your design:

- thrives when there is fluidity and spontaneity in daily life
- works well with loose and flexible routines and structures
- prospers when you use your intuition to plan out your days and have a general sense of your weekly commitments and structure
- rigid expectations and goals will not work well with this design
- make sure to plan in "nothing days" and try not to overcommit
- If you try to force yourself to follow a strict structure, you will unconsciously be moving towards the edge of your Window of Tolerance and into a Dysregulated Unaligned State.

**Left Facing:**

If your Digestion arrow is left facing, your design:

- thrives when there's structure & consistency
- predictability & repetivitiveness is your friend
- is energetically matched to having mapped out schedules and routines
- structured meal plans and schedules work well with your design
- If you don't plan ahead and/or follow a consistent routine, you will unconsciously be moving towards the edge of your Window of Tolerance.

The moment that you align yourself correctly in terms of what is environmentally correct for you, you immediately, along with the obvious of strategy and authority, are beginning to align yourself to the correct perspective.

-

But you cannot take advantage of the unique perspective if you're not in the right place looking at the right things. It's not going to do you any good.

———

— RA URU HU

# HD
# ENVIRONMENTS

......................................

In Human Design, your unique Environment influences how you feel in a range of environments and gives you some insight into the type of space that your body resonates best with and in turn nurtures and grounds your Nervous System. Keep in mind that our 'Environment' can be thought of as a physical place and also as a concept. As we experience our Saturn's Return, our astrological coming of age which occurs around the ages of 27 to 30, our Environment starts to become more important to focus on because we are entering into our 'adulthood' phase of life.

**Your unique environment is a space where you...**

* feel less resistance in life and experiences
* feel more aligned, safe and "in flow"
* begin to notice and experience more opportunities for growth
* are less likely to take on outside conditioning

There are six _Environments_ split into two categories: Hardscapes & Landscapes

**Hardscapes:**

**Caves, Markets, & Kitchens**

If you have a Hardscape Environment, it is important to look at your immediate surroundings, work out what is available for you to use, and create spaces aligned with your Environment Archetype.

**Landscapes:**

**Mountains, Valleys, & Shores**

If you have a Landscape Environment, it is important to look at the transpersonal energy of your surroundings and how you feel in the space, the energy/vibrations it gives off.

The ultimate goal is to help our Nervous System feel safe enough to enter and stay in our Flow State, which then allows us to vibrate at a higher frequency and take aligned action. The following section will give you some insight into the type of space that your body resonates best with and in turn, nurtures and grounds your Nervous System. I have listed some ways and things you can experiment with when reviewing or creating a home and/or work environment that will support your Environment Archetype.

**Caves = all about feeling safe in your space**
- calming, soft and low-level lighting
- fewer windows are ideal or even covered by blinds when you feel like it etc.
- cooler temperature
- one main entrance into space
- angled towards or facing the entrance to the space
- secluded/private space or removed from the general area
- having your back to the wall
- exclusivity - only you or a select few people allowed into the space - some people may not be too worried about the exclusivity of there space.
- ability to close off the space or close the door

**Markets = all about the ability to choose who and what enters your live**
- a bustling environment filled with energy
- feels comforting yet stimulating
- possibly working in areas like your favourite cafes or communal spaces
- lots of things to look at
- a mixture of different textures, fabrics, colours, and smells
- possibly background noise or chatter
- your space needs to reflect your interests and your unique design choices
- places for other people to sit and relax/interact with you
- a feeling of exclusivity in your home - choosing who can enter

## Kitchens = all about alchemy

- a creative and inspiring space
- background noises can be helpful
- living in an area or space which is rich with diversity
- a central gathering space where you are in the middle of the action but can move to the side when needed
- co-working spaces or working from an area that is in a central location in your home - dining room table/ kitchen bench
- ability to talk to others and bounce ideas off people
- making your space unique and distinctly your own
- using lots of different smells and textures in the space

## Mountains = all about vantage points

- possibly literally living or working somewhere high up
- working in front of windows with views of the outside environment
- working in large, well-lit, open spaces
- using air purifiers
- using fans or open windows allowing the air to blow onto you
- a feeling of coziness yet the ability to see what is happening around you
- lots of plants around and/or consistent trips to natural environments to reflect on your perspectives on things
- the ability to "get out of town" to rest and recoup

**Valleys = all about intimacy & acoustics**

- living or working on ground level - possibly close to nature or spaces where there are things going on around you
- possible small and narrow spaces - small rooms/nooks, or working in alleyway cafes etc.
- possibly working off to the side, tucked into a corner in large environments
- spaces where you can people watch and listening to what is happening outside - cars going by, hearing conversations as people walk by, natural sounds
- influences of outside acoustics - the ability to hear what's happening around you can choosing whether or not to engage
- lots of natural influences and plants
- possibly unwinding with reality TV or listening to podcasts discussing others and social topics
- using air purifiers or opening windows for fresh air

**Shores = all about boundaries/perimeters**

- living or working near a place that has transition in landscape or physically see two areas come together - shoreline, rivers, ponds, next to the park, fences to street/sidewalk
- ability to landscape gaze - stargazing, watching the ocean etc.
- living and working in open spaces where you can see other adjoining rooms
- working by a window
- painting your rooms different colours to create a transitional element
- having set work and relaxation clothes - changing as soon as you get home
- trying not to bring work home - clear boundaries of on and off time
- using nightlights to mark transition of rooms in the darkness

# HD
# EMOTIONAL CENTER

....................................

In Human Design, The Solar Plexus is both an Emotional Awareness Center as well as being a Motor/Energy Center. Its motor generates emotions in a wave pattern, moving us from highs to lows and back to highs again. These emotional waves have a huge impact on us as individuals and as a whole society. Every gate within this center has to do with how we feel, process, and express our emotions. It is also home to our Nervous System and also the center that is most susceptible to outside influences and conditioning.

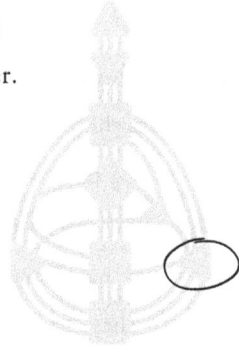

The Solar Plexus is by far the most important center in Human Design in my opinion. It is part of the foundational elements which everything else is built upon regarding our Emotional Intelligence, our ability to regulate our Nervous System, and our Manifesting abilities. It is also the Center of Spiritual Awareness as our emotions are what help us tune into spirit and the universe.

Take a look at the Human Design chart you generated earlier for yourself. If you have a black or coloured in Solar Plexus, it means you have a Defined Emotional Center. Meaning - you have access to a consistent way of moving through, processing, generating, and emitting emotional energy.

If your Solar Plexus is white or not coloured in, it means that you have an Undefined Emotional Center and an inconsistent way of processing Solar Plexus energy.

# UNDEFINED
# SOLAR PLEXUS

..................................

People who have an Undefined Solar Plexus are true empaths. They have the gift to empathise with others and lean into their emotions, which can be both a blessing and a curse as they can take on the emotional energy, even the emotional baggage, of others seeing as the centre is Undefined.

People who have an Undefined Solar Plexus can also magnify the feelings and emotions they have taken on within themselves - they feel them more intensely. Sometimes, they can be labelled as being emotionally unstable or highly emotional/sensitive because of this.

Seeing as they don't have consistent access to this center's energy, they don't process emotions consistently and can spend a fair amount of time processing and feeling the emotions of others. They still do have to ability to generate their own emotions though. When they take on other people's emotions as their own, it severely affects their ability to stay within their Window of Tolerance and in a holistically Aligned Nervous System State.

The Undefined Solar Plexus' challenge in life is to learn how to observe other people's emotions without taking on and amplifying them.

**How to work with having an Undefined Solar Plexus**

- ask yourself if the emotion you are feeling is your own or if have you picked it up from someone else
- ask yourself if you are in the Solar Plexus' "Not-Self" traits of avoiding confrontation, escaping strong emotions, or self-blame when you feel like you are being too sensitive or emotional
- try to allocate some alone time each day/week to rest, recoup and restore your emotional energy levels

- when you are feeling overwhelmed by emotions, try a grounding practice or breathing/Vagus Nerve exercise to access some of the soothing parasympathetic energy to help move you back into Ventral flow

- you can discharge some of the extra emotional energy around you by shaking out your arms and legs, intuitively moving your body, going for a walk etc.

- create and hold strong physical and energetic boundaries around yourself and your emotional energy

- brainstorm situations, experiences, topics or people that zap your energy and either cut them out or reduce the amount of exposure you have to them (Stop watching the news, unfollow people on social media etc.)

- remove yourself from situations or from others who are giving off unhealthy emotional vibes that can emotionally drain you and pull you into a low-frequency Survival Stress State (Fight/Flight/Freeze)

- try not to avoid confrontation and become afraid of other people's emotions because of the impact it may have on you. Possibly look at timing your challenging conversations etc. when your or the other party/ies are not at the highest or lowest point in their emotional wave

- try to detach yourself from other people's emotions so that you can support them rather than trying to fix their emotions (which can be hard to master as an empath.)

- make decisions based on your Sacral, Splenic or Lunar Authority (unless your Authority is Emotional) rather than your current emotional state

- try to remember that you don't have a consistent way of working with your emotions however you have conditioned reactions, emotional patterns, and ways of processing emotions based on your upbringing

# DEFINED
# SOLAR PLEXUS

· · · · · · · · · · · · · · · · · · · · · · · · · · · · · · ·

People who have a Defined Emotional Center will have Emotional Authority. The majority of humanity has Emotional Authority as their Inner Authority. Their outside world doesn't have too much effect on their emotions yet Defined Solar Plexus people have a great influence on the emotions and feelings of the people around them.

Someone who has a Defined Solar Plexus needs to take time to come to a decision. The bigger the decision the longer they need to take. This waiting period helps them to feel all their emotions in the wave and gain clarity. If they do not take time to ride the emotional wave, their rash decisions can backfire causing stress and can put a strain on their Nervous System's ability to stay in a Regulated Aligned State.

People who have a Defined Solar Plexus need to ensure they feel and release all their emotions. This can be a challenge for some as they may be been conditioned growing up to repress their emotions. The act of repressing not only causes strain on their Nervous Systems and mental health but can also cause physical ailments. The other way conditioning can affect them is if they were taught to look outwards to make decisions instead of trusting their own emotional authority.

**How to work with having a Defined Solar Plexus**

- practice patience - ride your emotional wave and feel all the emotions to be felt until they mellow out then act
- remember that 100% emotional clarity usually isn't possible. Anything above 70% certainty can be deemed as reaching clarity

- try not to decode and interpret your emotions using logic as it can become confusing to you. Emotions are meant to be felt

- give yourself time to make decisions and reach emotional clarity rather than making spontaneous and quick decisions in the heat of the moment

- possibly reframe the belief that you can be indecisive. You're not... you just need more time to reach a decision when your emotional wave evens out.

- Use the phrases: "Can I get back to you?" "Let me think about it." I'm going to sleep on it before I make up my mind."

Our brain and the state of our Nervous System are a direct reflection of all the experiences we have had in our lives thus far.  Thanks to a thing called neuroplasticity, we can rewire our brains and cultivate a healthier Nervous System and higher Emotional Intelligence by changing, reorganising, or growing neural networks via 'Top Down' & 'Bottom Up' Strategies.

Turns out we can teach an old dog new tricks.

———

— EVA HATTIN

# NINE

......................................

# HOW TO MOVE
# BACK INTO FLOW

There are two ways to help strengthen and work with our Autonomic Nervous System to move back into Flow and attract higher frequency things and desires.

There's the Bottom Up Approach:

- Focusing on helping our Autonomic Nervous System feel safe and strengthening the Vagus Nerve via bodywork and energy clearing.

& then there's the Top Down Approach:

- Focusing on becoming consciously aware of and rewiring thoughts and belief patterns (think mindset work), as well as identifying Safety and Danger Signs; removing or reducing Danger Signs etc.

The most effective way to influence and 'heal' our Nervous System is with a predominately "Bottom Up" approach. This is because the Automatic Nervous System determines how safe we are, via Neuroception, which then determines how we feel and act well and truly before conscious thought. Our Nervous System needs to feel safe enough for us to move back into an Aligned Regulated State.

Bottom Up techniques help work through stress and trauma that is stored in the body. It can accomplish 'healing,' restoring the baseline state back to Regulation, and moving back into the holistic Flow State 'faster' compared to the same amount of Top Down talk-therapy & mindset work.

Don't get me wrong, talk therapy & mindset work do have their place (initially, a Top-Down approach is needed to help identify Safety and Danger signs etc.) but, the body needs to feel safe enough for the Top-Down strategies to be highly effective.

By combining both the Bottom-Up and Top-Down approaches, we can work towards strengthening our Nervous System and moving into a higher frequency.

..................................

# BEFORE YOU BEGIN

Remember, growth isn't linear. Things will happen, our needs and states will change. Take a look through the following sections to get a idea of the resources, professionals, and strategies that are available to help strengthen your Vagus Nerve and help with Nervous System Regulation. After viewing all the resources, we will work together to map out a stage by stage implementation self-care plan tailored to your unique needs and specific Nervous System state.

When we are aware of and use the right resources for our Nervous System State, we will be able to:

- move back into Regulated Alignment quicker and easier
- create and adapt our Nervous System self-care rituals and practices that have the most bang for their buck
- increase the tone of our Vagus Nerve
- gently widen our Window of Tolerance
- able to manifest and take aligned action with ease
- spend more time being holistically aligned and in a high-frequency state
- begin to attract and invite in desires and things that match our mental state or mindset

# IN THE MOMENT
# QUICK GUIDE

....................................

## If I am feeling:

### On edge or experiencing sensory overload I can:

- move my body
- stand or sit up with spine extended - one hand on heart the other on stomach - taking full deep breaths
- bring awareness to the rhythmic pattern of my breaths/movement in my body

### Stressed or overwhelmed I can:

- move my body
- stand or sit up with my spine extended
- bring awareness to my current environment. - scan the environment, naming the objects you see from left to right
- shake my arms and legs, rub my hands together - or intuitively move my body

### Angry:

- apply deep body pressure
- taking deep full breaths while pushing my hands against the wall or each other Bringing awareness to pressure in my hands, arms, chest - moving all the way down to the grounding pressure on my feet
- 'Voo' breathing - deep breaths - feeling the vibration as you make the loud sound Voo on exhales ( See breathing exercises on page 138)
- bringing more awareness to the grounding pressure on my feet - rolling them back and forth or shifting my weight to vary pressure/sensations on feet

### Anxious

- apply deep body pressure - self bear hug, weighted blanket, squeezing up and down my arms/legs
- taking regular slow breaths - not breathing too deeply
- bringing awareness to my current environment. - scan the environment, naming the objects you see from left to right

# If I am feeling:

## Panicked or frozen I can:
- apply deep body pressure - self bear hug, weighted blanket, squeezing up and down arms/legs
- bringing awareness to the pressure on my feet as I walk
- taking slow, full breaths
- bringing awareness to my current environment. - scan the environment, naming the objects you see from left to right
- slowly shaking or jumping with my breath - landing on your exhales

## Disconnected or burnt out I can:
- slow down or stop the activity I am doing
- apply deep pressure on body - squeezing hands together, crossing my arms over each other and then squeezing my way down my arms
- using my hands to squeeze down legs and calves
- bring all my attention to my body as I walk - focus on how each movement of my legs, ankles, and feet feel - how my hips and arms move. - use varying pressure/pace and gaits while noticing how the sensations feel in my body

# IF I AM IN FIGHT/FLIGHT MOBILISING ENERGY

.....................................

To bring back into Aligned Regulation (Ventral) from Fight/Flight- I need to move my body to release the build-up of stress hormones and/or ground myself in the moment. This will shift me back into a higher frequency.

I am feeling: anxious; angry; stressed; on edge; overstimulated/overwhelmed

Techniques or strategies:

- rubbing your hands together vigorously
- extension of the spine - standing or sitting tall
- making physical contact with your face, neck, chest, arms, and legs (touching or gently squeezing)
- movements that feel safe and grounding - gentle walks, swaying
- shaking body, hands, arms, and/or legs to release the mobilising energy
- rocking or swaying from side to side
- intuitively moving your body
- dancing
- laughing or watching comedy
- creative activities - painting, sewing, writing, clay work etc.
- humming
- 'Voo' Breathing (Breathing in - Releasing through the mouth making an audible 'Voo' fog horn sound - See page 138)
- slow, full, even breaths
- deep pressure - pushing hands against the wall while noticing sensations, bear hugs with others or yourself

- bringing awareness to contact points of your feet on the ground – feeling the sensation of feet on the ground as you shift your weight; rock back and forth while pressing your feet into the ground.

- bringing awareness to your current environment. - scan the environment, naming the objects you see from left to right

- sitting down and bringing awareness to your pelvis and bum; rock and wiggle hips and notice the anchoring sensations through your pelvic floor and hips.

- centring activity: place one hand on the heart and one hand on the belly. Bring your awareness to the weight/pressure on your body; Sense the weight of the hands on the torso, feel the coolness or warmth of your hands, and bring some awareness to your breathing rate - feel how your hands rise and fall in sync with your breath.

# IF I AM IN FREEZE
# IMMOBILISING ENERGY

..................................

To bring back into Aligned Regulation (Ventral) from Freeze - I need to interrupt the feedback loop using sensory tools and ground myself in the moment.

I am feeling: highly anxious; numb; shutdown; depressive feelings; "out of it"

Techniques or strategies:

- slowing down or stopping the activity you are doing - leaving the situation, resting and alone time if possible

- connection- calling trusted Safety Sign person - preferably face time for eye contact which helps the Vagus Nerve.

- connection - co-regulating with a Safety Sign person or animal - hugs, taking natural breaths near each other and "borrowing" their Regulation (Ventral) to help you centre yourself and shift into a higher frequency

- visualising your Safety Sign person or pet

- take a few short sharp inhale breaths, to get some mobilising energy, followed by some full deep breaths

- sensory: using essential oils or 'safety sign' scents like perfume etc. to ground yourself

- sensory defences - remove self from the sensory trigger - sunglasses; putting headphones (with or without Safety Sign music) or earbuds in, closing blinds; change into comfortable clothes; warm drinks; heat packs etc.

- bilateral eye movements - keeping your head as still as possible while facing forwards- scan your eyes across space from left/right; up/down, in slow circles while taking natural breaths

- body scan ( See page 113)

- sleep

- deep pressure - hugging yourself; squeezing up and down arms/legs. If sitting, try to push your knees together using your hands while resisting the movement with your legs

- bringing awareness to your current environment. - scan the environment, naming the objects you see from left to right, looking for 'safety signs'

- bring all your attention to your body as you walk - focus on how each movement of your legs, ankles, and feet feel - how your hips and arms move. - use varying pressure/pace and gaits while noticing how the sensations feel in the body

- bring awareness to the contact points of your feet on the ground – focus on adding more pressure to the ball of your foot or pressing your feet into the ground.

If you want to manage your emotions better, your brain gives you two options: You can learn to regulate them from the top down or from the bottom up.

———

BESSEL A. VAN DER KOLK

# TOP DOWN STRATEGIES

...............................

A Top Down Strategy focuses on becoming consciously aware of and rewiring thoughts and belief patterns via Neuroplasticity (think - mindset work and priming your Reticular Activating System for abundance), as well as identifying Safety and Danger Signs; removing or reducing Danger Signs etc.

# SPECIALISED SUPPORT
# FOR YOUR VAGUS NERVE

......................................

- Acupuncture
- Allergy and Immunology
- Chiropractor
- Craniosacral Therapy
- Dietician
- Doctor/GP
- Domestic Violence/Abuse hotlines and community support networks
- Doula / Postpartum Doula
- Greif & Loss Hotline and community support networks
- HeartMath - heartmath.org
- Hydrotherapy
- Kinesiologist
- Lactation & Breastfeeding Consultants
- Massage Therapist – Gentle Pressure (Fight/Flight) & Harder Pressure (Freeze)
- Mental Health Hotlines & community services
- Naturopath
- OBGYN
- Occupational Therapist - Helps with Executive Functioning (See page 126)
- Optometrist
- Physiotherapist
- Reflexology
- Therapist, Psychologist etc.
- Sensory Deprivation Pods – Magnesium/Epsom Salt Soaks
- Sleep Study

# ALTERNATIVE THERAPIES

·····························

- Aura Cleansing
- Binaural beats
- Breathwork
- Brown Noise
- Burning incense
- Chakra cleanse
- Charging & working with crystals
- Chinese Medicine
- Cleansing space with salt
- Clearing clutter & airing out home
- EFT Tapping - Emotional Freedom Techniques (See page 117)
- Energy Clearing/Cleansing
- Equine-assisted Therapy (Horses)
- Essential oils (See page 175)
- Grounding
- Hydrotherapy
- Hypnotherapy
- Neurolinguistic Programming
- Reiki
- Sacred Medicine
- Smudging or Saging
- Sound baths
- Therapy Dog or Animal
- Timeline Therapy & Akashic Records
- White Noise

# BASIC NEEDS
# SELF-ASSESSMENT

........................................

In order to help our Autonomic Nervous System feel safe enough to leave survival mode, heal, and move back into Alignment, we need to be in an environment and nurture a lifestyle where our essential basic needs are met. I have included a self-assessment to work through, journal or reflect on.

We need to make sure we are nurturing our:

- Physiological needs ( nutritious food, water, shelter, health)
- Safety needs (stability, secure home, workplace and family environment)
- Social needs (positive safe connections & support)
- Self-esteem, Emotion & Comfort needs
- Cognitive needs (things that bring us joy)
- Spiritual needs

## Self-assessment:

- Do I feel safe in my home?
- Does my home décor and layout bring me joy?
- Does my home and/or workspace remain relatively clutter-free?
- Do I feel safe in my relationship?
- Do my family/friends honour, recognise and appreciate the work I do/mental load? If not, have I asked them for help/implemented a system to reduce my mental load?
- Do I feel safe at my place of work?
- Do I usually get enough sleep?
- Do I usually eat something fresh and unprocessed every day?
- Do I drink enough water each day?
- Do I feel comfortable in the clothes I have?

- Do I spend time each week in nature, no matter how briefly?

- Do I get enough sunlight – especially in the morning?

- Do I see my doctor at least once a year for a check-up?

- Do I see a dentist every six months?

- Do I get enough intimate time with my partner?

- Do I get enough wanted physical contact and connection?

- Do I get enough time to socialise outside of my home with friends and family?

- Do I have friends or family I can call when I am down, friends/family who listen?

- Can I honestly ask for help when I need it?

- Do I get enough alone time?

- Do I get enough fun exercise?

- Do I do things that give me a sense of fulfilment, joy and purpose?

- Do I regularly release negative emotions?

- Do I frequently clear my space and body energetically?

- Do I listen to and follow my intuitive nudges?

- Do I set aside time to connect with spirit/the universe etc each day?

- Do I take on other peoples energy without realising?

- Do I need to set any boundaries with others or energetically?

- Are there things I can do, change, or ask for to make sure my basic needs are met?

# LIMITING BELIEFS
# REFELCTION TOOL

. . . . . . . . . . . . . . . . . . . . . . . . . . . . . .

This tool can be used in conjunction with the Personal Nervous System States Blueprint on page 45 but can also be used as journal prompts. What is the belief/s that came up when you mapped out your blueprint? (Aligned Flow State, Fight/Flight/Freeze State)

Reflective questions:

- Why am I burnt out? Am I not setting or holding boundaries? Do I need more support/help?
- Am I feeling guilt or shame around my choices? Who is guilting/shaming me?
- Am I feeling judged for choices? Who is judging me?
- Am I feeling judged for how I act or hold myself?
- Why do I fear having a lack of control over the situation?
- Why do I feel like I am not a good/ good enough? Who told me that?
- Why do I feel like I'm going to fail? Who is the person making that judgement? Is it me or an outside influence?
- Why do I feel like I have no help? Have I asked? Am I afraid to ask? Why don't I trust them to help?
- Why do I feel like I don't know what I am doing? Am I spending time around people or consuming media that is toxic/sugar coating etc. Who can I turn to for honest, nonjudgment advice?
- Why do I feel like it's not safe to take inspired action or calculated risks? Can there be precautions put in place to help me to feel safe?
- Is there a childhood trauma (mine or ancestors) influencing my thoughts?
- I feel like it's not safe to trust other people. Where is this thought stemming from?

- How does this lack of control or safety make me feel? Blamed, guilted, shamed, misunderstood, disrespected, excluded, sad, tense, anxious, hurt etc.?
- What values, attitudes and beliefs around money, wealth creation or manifestation did I grow up with? Do I agree with them?
- What ones would I change?
- What beliefs do I have around people with money and wealth?
- What feelings come up when I think about handling large sums of money?
- What fears do I have about attaining the desires I am manifesting?
- What societal, cultural or racial influences are affecting me?

## I like to use this questioning process when I am working through my limiting beliefs:

- **What is the belief that came up or the core message?**

- **Is it true? Am I 100% certain this is the case? Can I find proof of this?**

- **Where is this belief stemming from?**
  *Society, People, Memories, Inherited or Instilled beliefs from childhood?*

- **What bodily sensations am I feeling when I think about those beliefs?**
  *Is it my Nervous System in survival mode - is it trying to protect me?*

- **What is stopping me from letting go of those beliefs?**
  *Again, Is it my Nervous System in survival mode - is it trying to protect me?*

- **What would I feel like and my life look like if I were to let those limiting beliefs go? Can I let them go? How can I release what no longer serves me?**

- **Who would I be or what would I be doing if I wasn't living with those beliefs anymore? Can I embody this now?**

- **How would this then impact how I am as an individual?**

# STRATEGIES FOR OPTIMISING YOUR VAGAL TONE

..................................

Social connection & Coregulation

- Connect with Safety Sign people and "borrow" their Regulation. This can be face-to-face or via technology. You will get better results when there is eye connection with each other. Laughter and fun are the best medicine. Cuddling and/or having some other kind of body contact with your safety sign person (holding hands, sitting next to them etc.) or pets all help with coregulation & positive social connection.

Nutrition

- See your doctor, dietician, and/or nutritionist to help develop a personalised plan. On page 118, you will find some nutritional information that has been shown to support our nervous systems

- Gentle Exercise - Consult with your doctor before attempting exercises.

- Vagal Exercises - See page 146

- Breathing Exercises  - See page 138

- Gargling excessively/loudly

- Consciously gagging with your toothbrush

- Loud humming, singing, chanting

Cold Exposure - Consult with your doctor before attempting cold exposure.

- Dunking face into ice water baths or splashing face with cold water
- Rubbing ice on face and lips
- Drinking cold iced water or cold drinks
- Placing an ice pack on your forehead or chest while resting
- Sucking on an ice cube or ice block
- Cold Showers
- Jumping into cold pool or ocean

Massage

- Vagal Face Massage See page 157
- Vagal Ear Massage - See page 153
- Feet/ Reflexology Points - See page 160

Screen Use:

- Limiting amount of time eyes are converging, looking up close to the screen, as it can move us into Fight/Flight (Sympathetic). Take regular screen breaks during the day and look away from your screen often.

# DAILY ACTIVITIES FOR SPECIFIC SURVIVAL STATES

......................................

The following activities can help shift you from Out-of-Alignment back into Flow as well as help strengthen your Nervous System.

All activities and suggestions in these sections:

- Quick Guide - Regulation Strategies - See page 92
- In the Moment Guide - Regulation Strategies - See page 94
- Vagal Tone sections - See page 109

**Additional Activities:**

For those in Fight/Flight Sympathetic, daily if possible:

- Gentle movement and exercise or slow walks – overexerting moves you out of your Window of Tolerance/increases stress
- Shaking and dancing out excess mobilising energy
- Deep, slow breathing
- Balance Exercises - standing on one foot, on a raised yoga block, balance beam/walking along the curb etc.

For those in Freeze Dorsal, daily if possible:

- Holding a power yoga pose for 60sec can be enough input for a day (Warrior 2, Tree, Goddess, Reclined Butterfly, Chair, Triangle, Child's pose etc.)
- Deep pressure – deep hugs from a safety person, self-hugs, weighted blankets
- Gentle intuitive stretching
- Short sharp breaths followed by easy deep breaths
- EFT Tapping
- Grounding exercises

# GROUNDING USING OUR FELT SENSES

....................................

The concept of Felt Senses came from Philosopher Eugene Gendlin. Basically, it's a physical experience we have. It's a bodily awareness of things, situations, people and/or events. It can also be thought of as bringing awareness inside our body in a certain situation and using that awareness to select specific strategies to help move back into Alignment/ Regulation (Ventral State).

We will focus on two main types of felt senses: Exteroception & Interoception

**Exteroception** is the sensitivity to stimuli outside the body; anything perceived by the 5 senses: sight, sound, touch, taste and smell. Exteroceptive grounding focuses on noticing some aspect of our external world to help move back into the Ventral Regulated Flow State.

**Interoception** is the sensitivity to stimuli inside our body via automatic processes (breathing/heart rate; digestion; muscle tension etc.) Interoceptive grounding focuses on noticing and changing some aspect of our internal processes to help move back into the Ventral Regulated State.

The following pages contain activities to help ground ourselves using our felt senses of Exteroception and Interoception.

## Scanning

- Identify 3 things in your environment that you are drawn to. (Flowers, cushions, clouds etc.)
- Identify 1 sensation you're aware of from within your body. when observing the things in the environment.
- Identify 3 more things you're drawn to in your environment.
- Take 3 Deep full breaths
- Notice what's happening now: How do you feel overall?

## Safety Sign

- Think of an Safety Sign item, experience or person that makes you feel safe & happy (Your partner, your pet, a family member, clothing item, song etc.)
- Identify the sensations and thoughts you have when you are thinking of it/them.
- What is the size, shape, textures, movements, or even colour are associated with this sensation or thought?
- Bring awareness to how you are now feeling compared to how you were feeling at the beginning.

## Other Mental Grounding Activities:

### Categories

- Name as many things as you can think of in a certain category.

### Sounds

- Focus on identifying and listening to a specific sound, neutral conversation, or voice around you.

### Counting

- Counting in number sequences. For example, the number of signs you see, the number of steps there are etc.

## Body Scan

- See page 113, for information about conducting a Body Scan

## Tuning In Breathing:

- See page 138, for Breathing Exercises

## Hand Clenches

- Clench both of your fists and hold them for 30 seconds, while taking slow deep breaths. Bring awareness to where you feel tension, resistance, and relief in your body when holding on and letting go.

## Hand Stretches

- Stretch your fingers as wide apart as you can and hold them for 30 seconds, while bringing awareness to where you feel tension, resistance, relief, stretching etc.
- Stretch your fingers as wide apart as you can and hold them for 30 seconds while bringing awareness to the muscle & webbing between you thumb and index finger.

## Spinal Twist Stretches

- Sit in a comfortable chair and place both of your hands on the left side of the chair
- Gently rotate your body to the left as far as possible - stopping when you feel discomfort
- Hold for 30 seconds while taking several deep breaths. Repeat the exercise to the right.

## Digging Heels Into The Ground

- Push/apply more pressure to both of your feet and hold them for 15 seconds while taking slow deep breaths. Bring awareness to where you feel tension, resistance, relief when letting go etc.

# BODY SCAN ACTIVITY

· · · · · · · · · · · · · · · · · · · · · · · · · · · · · ·

01    Lie down or sit in a comfortable position and close your eyes if it feels safe to do so.

02    Bring awareness to the top of your head and then slowly move your focus to the different parts of your body as you move your attention down to your feet. The aim is to notice the pain, tension, weakness, stiffness throughout your body etc. and not to change anything just yet. We are being a gentle observer.

03    Mentally or physically note & select an option (using the following pages) where and what sensations you came across. See the example below.

04    To end, scan your whole body as one piece instead of individually. Notice a place in your body where it feels comfortable to feel the movement of your breath. Focus on this spot and take three breaths, feeling the comfortable sensations in that part of the body.

05    Reflect on the areas you made note of. What is it telling you? What does it need? More movement, tension release, stillness, warmth etc.?

**tired,**
**overwhelmed,**
**tense jaw**

**tight shoulders**

**eg. Notes on Body**
**Scan**

**hungry**
**bloated**

**lower back pain**

**right knee pain**

**cold feet**

# BODY SCAN

**Date:**

**Time:**

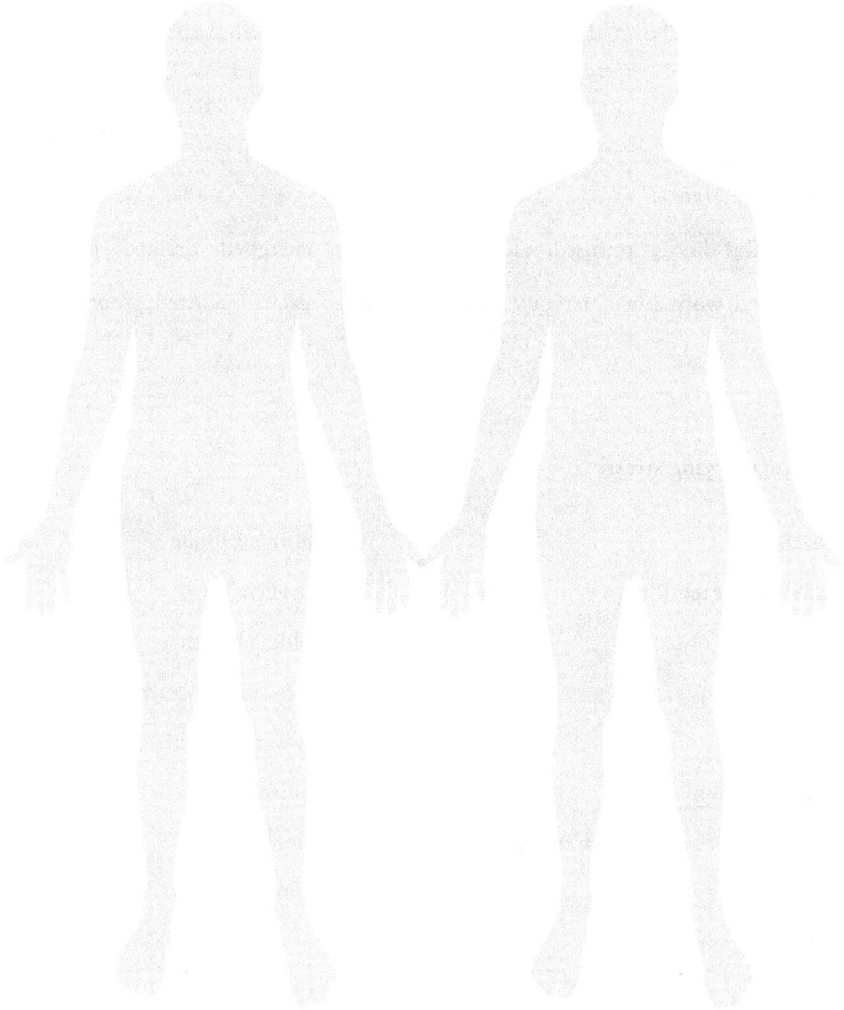

FRONT                    BACK

# BODY SCAN

**Body:**

aches, pain, bloated, gas, breathless, strong, chills, Goosebumps, pins and needles, tingling, numb, flushed, cold, warm, sweaty, clammy, trembling, shaky, itchy, tense, tight, relaxed, sore, sharp pain, dull pain, deep sighs, knotted stomach, butterflies, stiff, weak, sore, heavy, light

**Emotional & Mental**

tired, numb, dizzy, confused, alert, calm, happy, energised, drained, joyful, faint overwhelmed, worn down, nervous, anxious, nauseated, excited, centred, grounded

**How I am carrying stress?**

| | |
|---|---|
| Headaches | Chronic Fatigue |
| Neck/Shoulder tension | Fibromyalgia |
| Clenching jaw | Holding breath |
| Teeth grinding | Short/Rapid breaths |
| Racing heart | Lower Back pain |
| Butterflies in stomach | Stomach pain |
| Needing to use the bathroom frequently | Voice or throat |
| Clenching fist | Insomnia |
| Sweaty or clammy palms | |

# EFT: EMOTIONAL FREEDOM TECHNIQUE - "TAPPING"

....................................

Emotional Freedom Techniques (EFT Tapping) was developed in the 1990's by Gary Craig, a Stanford Engineer who worked for the founder of Thought Field Therapy, Dr. Roger Callahan. It can be thought of as a psychological version of acupuncture/acupressure. EFT involves focusing on a specific issue or mindset you would like to work through and resolve while using your fingertips to tap on certain acupuncture/acupressure points on the hands, face and body.

You conduct the tapping in a specific sequence while working through the specific issue or mindset that is bothering you. There are a range of practitioners specialising in EFT courses and sessions as well as free resources available on the internet for you to explore.

# NUTRITION

........................................

**NUTRITIONAL DISCLAIMER:**

This information is designed for general informational purposes only and not a prescription. Before you change your diet and/or add supplements etc., discuss your health and concerns with your doctor or health practitioner. They will be able to do a complete health physical and will help you make an informed decision based on your current needs.

The following section contains information about food, nutrients, vitamins and minerals that have been shown to possibly help decrease the level of physical/physiological inflammation in your body, following chronic stress, as well as have shown evidence to assist with the Myelination of nerves.

# NUTRITION

............................................

The information below assists restore & aide a healthy gut microbiome and reduces the effect of stress & inflammation in the gut. They are high in nutrients, phytonutrients, antioxidants, fibre, & low GI.

- Eat whole foods (fresher and less processed food. Organic, where possible, is even better)
- Consume fruit in moderate amounts as it's high in sugar

Try to include more non-starchy vegetables in your diet.

- Artichoke
- Asparagus
- Beans & Bean sprouts
- Beets
- Brussels sprouts
- Broccoli
- Cabbage (green, bok choy, Chinese)
- Capsicum (Peppers)
- Carrots
- Cauliflower
- Sweet Potato
- Corn
- Peas

**Grains** can be a problem for some following chronic stress

**Legumes:** Soaked overnight to make them more gut-friendly

**Meat:** grass-fed or organic beef, pork, lamb & cage-free chicken (less fatty & less modified to help with gut better balance/ratio of omega-6 to omega-3 compared to modified products)

**Fish:** Sustainably Sourced - anti-inflammatory omega-3 fatty acids

**Eggs:** Cage free and organic if possible

**Dairy:** Lactose might cause a problem with the microbiome in the gut after chronic stress. You could try removing it for a few months (consult with your doctor first) and reintroduce it with probiotic yoghurts. Possibility of using plant-based milk or even Goat/Sheep based milk if there is a Cow's Milk Protein Allergy

**Refined Sugar:** avoid if possible
Alternatives: use organic/raw honey, maple syrup etc.

**Oils:** extra virgin olive oil, avocado oil, sesame seed oil. Other types of oils can lead to inflammation because of the high Omega 6s, baked oils are often hydrogenised and become trans fats.

**Fermented foods:** can help with gut health - Kefir, Kombucha, Miso, Tempeh etc.

**Supplements:**
Specific Vitamins/Minerals found in Unprocessed Whole food groups. Check with your doctor before starting or stopping supplements. Have them create a plan or a multivitamin selection based on your specific needs. Try to get these primarily through your food/diet instead of through supplements.
*Omega 3's; Vitamin D (Including safe sun exposure); Iron (Vitamin C aids iron absorption); Vitamin B6 & B12; Turmeric; Zinc; Selenium; Melatonin; Probiotics; Choline; Lecithin; Glycine*

# SLEEP

..............................

- Try to get the maximum amount of sleep possible. (More so for people who have an altered baseline state and are living in Fight, Flight or Freeze)
- If struggling to sleep/ fall back asleep: use an Online Sleep Calculator to try and wake up at the end of a sleep cycle. You will feel much better waking at the end of a sleep cycle than in the middle of one.
- If possible, nap when you feel tired.
- For parents, tag team with your partner or a 'Safety Sign' person so that you can sleep in/nap.

**Setting up your bed for sleep success**

- Make it as cosy and comfortable as possible – linen sheets, the right pillow for your sleep needs, dark room, possibly use an eye mask, using lavender room spray and magnesium body spray before bed, using white noise machine, angling night light so that it isn't shining directly into your eyes
- Create a personalised bedtime/winddown routine.
- Opening the blinds on waking to help regulate circadian rhythms
- Get some sunlight during the day.
- Limiting screen time and harsh lighting before bed.
- Try not to exercise before bed –gentle stretching or yoga poses are okay.

# MEDITATION

...................................

For those whose Neuroception has determined that meditating is a Danger Sign, try some of the following suggestions:

**Meditations with anchoring sound –**

- use a white/brown noise machine, a calming soundtrack, a sound bath, or rain sounds or following along a guided meditation from the internet

**Meditations with a Safety Sign -**

**Breaths:**

- using natural breaths vs. deep breathing as deep breathing may make you feel worse/hyperventilate if you are in Fight/Flight

**Scents:**

- using essential oils or specific perfumes

**Visual:**

- keeping your eyes open, placing Safety Signs in front of you, visualising safety signs/places, having a Safety Sign person with you

**Tactile:**

- comfortable cosy clothes, a soft blanket, heat pack over your lap or shoulders, cuddling a pet or blanket.

**Location:**

- meditating while lying down in bed, sitting in comfortable chair, sitting outside in nature

**Proprioception:**

- weighted blanket over you lap, pushing and releasing hands together, shifting your weight or sitting on a pillow or Shakti Mat while meditating, massaging hands or body while meditating

**Moving or rocking while meditating**

- moving while meditating can help release mobilising fight/flight stress energy and make it feel less uncomfortable. - Swaying, rocking, standing and walking around, stretching etc.

# MINDFUL ACTIVITIES

••••••••••••••••••••••••••••••

- Gratitude: Prime your Reticular Activating System. List things you are grateful for in the shower, while you are driving, brushing your teeth etc. These can be written, said aloud, or thoughts. If you get stuck, start with something small like "I am grateful for my body for ____; I am grateful for my eyesight because____: I am grateful for the roof over my head.... etc. and work your way up.

- Working with clay

- Process Art - not worrying about then end product - just exploring/ having fun

- Painting

- Drawing

- Colouring in

- Sewing, Knitting, Embroidery etc.

- Slow walks

- Easy bike rides

- Yoga/Pilates

- Sound Baths

- Cacao/Hot Chocolate/Chai Latte/ Tea

- Gardening

- Baths or foot soaks

- Self-massage with body/essential oils/body brushing

- Weekly at home facial/mud or hair masks etc.

- Intuitive Stretching

- Gentle breathing exercises

- Body Scan activity

- Meditation

- Lying down and listening to rain sounds/music/podcast

- Reading in a safe cosy spot

- Dancing

- Cooking or baking

- Gazing -Watching the ocean, fireplace/fire pit, clouds, rivers etc.

- Reiki

# EXECUTIVE FUNCTIONING

····································

Poor or dysfunctional Executive Functioning skills can play a huge role in our ability to stay in a holistically Aligned State. Harvard describes Executive function skills as "the mental processes that enable us to plan, focus attention, remember instructions, and juggle multiple tasks successfully. Just as an air traffic control system at a busy airport safely manages the arrivals and departures of many aircraft on multiple runways, the brain needs this skill set to filter distractions, prioritize tasks, set and achieve goals, and control impulses."

Executive Functioning involves:

- planning
- prioritising
- organising
- self-regulation
- impulse control
- working memory (holding several pieces of information in your brain at one time like following multistep processes)
- problem-solving
- task initiation
- flexible thinking (thinking about things in a new or different way)
- self-monitoring (monitoring and regulating emotions, behaviours, body language etc in social settings)

If any of these skills are weak or dysfunctional, it can create additional mental and emotional stress. It can also be the source of physical, mental, and visual clutter which then impacts our ability to stay Regulated as we can get overstimulated and overwhelmed by it and leave our Window of Tolerance.

Having weak or dysfunctional Executive Functioning skills can develop from a range of things:

- sleep deprivation
- chronic stress and burnout
- doing the Executive Functioning for both you and others (your children, partner, parents etc. - Planning, remembering, and organising for them etc.)
- growing up with parents or caregivers who have dysfunctional Executive Functioning skills
- specific Disorders such as ADHD and Dyslexia etc.
- differences in brain development and brain chemicals
- trauma and traumatic brain injuries

I have put together an example list of things that you could implement or bring more awareness to, to help with reducing your mental load and the toll on your Nervous System. An Occupational Therapist can help with Executive Functioning challenges.

**Planning, Organising, Memory & Time Management**

- Create daily and situational routines
- Central family calendar or use a synced digital calendar app with a list of important details and phone numbers
- Checklist or reusable checklists of tasks to complete
- Filling up with petrol the day before you have to go somewhere or when it gets halfway
- Brainstorm or brain dump all your thoughts, things that need to get done, want to do etc.
- If it can be done in 2 mins just do it
- If it's a big overwhelming task.... Set a timer for 5 or 10 mins. You can then stop or continue after the timer goes off... starting is the hardest part
- Use a timer or watch to remind you to hang out washing if the machine doesn't beep, to start dinner, to start your evening routine etc,
- Use cues - time of day dictates when you start dinner prep, time of day for walks etc.

**Meals**

- Create a central grocery list on the fridge - add to it as you notice things need to be bought/replenished.
- Create an easy menu for the week
- Create a cookbook or screenshot/ save a list of recipes to fall back on
- Meal plan and lunch plan - stick with easy staples and then branch out. Maybe Monday = chicken and three types of vegetables, Tuesday =sausages and salad, etc. routine

**Planning Ahead**

- Aim to leave 10-15 mins earlier to account for delays
- Sunday and/or nightly sit down or meetings with your partner about week plans/ important dates and appointments
- Plan what will likely occur and maybe challenges- think through how you would respond, and maybe plan for that by taking certain items like a small umbrella, premade coffee in a travel mug, snacks etc.
- To-do lists: sort into the categories of most important, can wait, or things to do later on.
- Backwards map trips or goals e.g. I have to be there at 10 am which means I need to leave by 9:20 am to get there and park the car, which means I need to be up by 7:30 etc.

**Systems**

- system for entering house... where do you take shoes off, leave your bag and keys? etc.

- systems for leaving the house - leave a checklist left on your bag to remind you to collect essential items before you leave or to remind you of specific meetings or tasks happening that day

- pack your bags and lunch the night before

- walk through your home to make sure everything is locked and turned off (Saying "The front door is locked" or "The hair straightener is unplugged" aloud before leaving can help with anxiety/memory)

- have a system so that you can shred, recycle or file paperwork as it comes into the house

- develop routines to leverage time – eg. watching TV while cooking/ironing, click and collect, grocery or meal delivery service

- outsourcing if possible- gardener, cleaner, hiring a professional organiser

- organise and cut up snack foods on Sunday so they are ready for the start of the week

- trying out using the "Kanban" organisational planning system

- store and take your grocery bags back to the car after putting away food

- have a system for laundry - two separate baskets to sort white and coloured clothing, having a rack or space to hang clothes that can be worn again, washing clothes on specific days etc.

**Working memory**

- create routines and systems
- write down important information & any information that requires you to remember more than one or two things
- write down thoughts or reminders before bed to help with sleep/daily tasks
- breakdown task into smaller bits and have additional breaks between completing task chucks
- slow down your days and routines as rushing causes problems with memory and information retrieval
- self-talk... "The door is locked"... "The hair straightener is unplugged."
- don't try to multitask... one task at a time unless you are leveraging time by watching TV and ironing etc.
- using checklist or notes
- have a home for everything in your house so that you can find it easily
- use mnemonics to help remember things
- visualise task steps or visualise where things are located

**For those with children:**

- Bath time routine... taking the change of clothes in, brushing teeth in bath or shower
- each night check the nappy bag and restock
- keep an umbrella, potty, towel, wipes, spare clothes, and soap (or soap sheets) in the back of the car for emergencies/ wipe down park slides etc.
- create or have a small snack platter of fruit and vegetables on offer while making dinner to stop interruptions and the "I'm Hungry"
- have a water bottle or designated cup for each child to minimise the number of dishes
- have a snack drawer in the fridge or cupboard with pre-cut foods ready to go.
- packing lunch and their bag the night before
- keep the pram in the car boot
- have two clothing options available for them to choose from. "Would you like to wear A or B?"
- have your kids help with toy storage solutions/home for each toy and create a pack-away routine. (It is beneficial for them to have a photo of what it should look like packed away for them to reference.
- have a photo or visual of their daily routine so they can know and prepare themselves for the day/what is coming up
- night-time or breakfast chats about what is happening tomorrow /today
- let them stay with you while they sus out and observe new settings/play areas until they feel comfortable to go off and play
- let them know in advance if anything changes to their daily routines
- create a toy rotation or even have storage tubs in the garage to store excess toys/dress-ups to cut down on visual stimulation
- have a dedicated art supplies section with the essentials and a dedicated art supplies section away from kids (glue/glitter/acrylic paints etc). Only put out/rotate a handful of supplies each week from the dedicated areas
- make it a game during transitions - who can hop/walk backwards/crawl to the bathroom etc.; Singing songs while cleaning up/putting on music to clean up too etc. Playing I spy as you get into the car or out of the car etc.

- Turning off screen time routine ("after this episode, the TV is going off" or give a 15min, 10min and 5 min countdown)
- System for entering house... where do they take shoes off, leave nappy bag, leave pram, put bags? etc. do they go and wash hands straight away... what can they do after?
- filling up with petrol while your partner is in the car with you to stay with the kids or have your partner fill up for you so you can stay at home with them
- have a specific towel design for each family member

# AFFIRMATIONS TO PRIME YOUR RETICULAR ACTIVATING SYSTEM

·····································

- My body and Nervous System are healthy and strong.
- I love and accept myself unconditionally.
- I am safe.
- I am strong.
- I am not in physical danger like my Nervous System believes. I am just emotionally uncomfortable. This will pass.
- My Nervous System will heal over time with self-care.
- I am learning to support myself according to my unique needs.
- I release the idea that I need to stay calm 24/7.
- All my emotions and feelings are valid.
- I inhale calm and release stress with each deep breath.
- My past holds no power over me.
- I worked through this emotion before and I can do it again.
- I give myself grace and time to figure out what strategies work best for my Nervous System.
- I am allowed to take it moment by moment and day by day.
- I honour my need for sleep and self-care.
- I am curious about my triggers and Danger signs.
- I am curious about the sensations in my body when I feel strong emotions.
- I am a money magnet.
- I am a powerful manifestor.
- It is safe to be loved.
- I am open to receiving love and support from others.
- I allow others to support me.
- I am worthy of massive compensation and abundance.
- People seek out and love to pay me.

**Human Design**

**Defined Solar Plexus**

- I allow myself time to rest, recoup and restore my energy levels.
- I honour my emotional waves.
- I allow and observe my emotions or feelings as they pass through the wave.
- I am intuitively connected to my emotions and feelings.
- All my emotions and feelings are valid and don't need to make sense.
- I trust the decision I make when I reach emotional clarity.
- I release the pressure to make on-the-spot decisions.
- Opportunities don't disappear if I do not immediately say yes. They will still be there when I reach emotional clarity.
- I make decisions when I am in a regulated, holistically aligned state.

**Undefined Solar Plexus**

- I trust the decisions I make in the moment.
- I acknowledge and release emotions that are not mine to process.
- I acknowledge and empathise with other people's emotions yet I am not obligated to help fix or make them feel better.
- I honour my need to rest, recoup and restore my energy levels.
- I hold strong emotional and energetic boundaries for myself.
- I trust my ability to remove myself from unhealthy or draining emotional situations.

# BOTTOM UP STRATEGIES

·····························

A Bottom Up Strategy Focusing on helping our Autonomic
Nervous System feel safe and strengthening the Vagus Nerve via
bodywork and energy clearing. In doing so, we are able to move
back into a higher frequency state and align our vibration to our
manifestations, goals and desires.

# SOMATIC MOVEMENTS

..................................

Somatic Movements are gentle movements & exercises that uses your mind-body connection to tune in to your body, look/listen to, and respond to the signals your body is sending to you: areas of pain, tension, imbalance, discomfort, weakness etc. Using this knowledge, and combining it with certain exercises & touch, can help you work toward releasing tension & strengthen your body & Nervous System.

- Breathing Exercises - See page 138

- Gentle Walking

- Acupressure & Acupuncture

- Intuitive stretching & dance

- Somatic Exercises (Slow & Calm Muscle Release Exercises)

- Progressive Muscle Relaxation

- Yoga

- Pilates

- Tai Chi

# BREATHING EXERCISES

.................................

**Tuning In Breathing:**

- Lie down in a comfortable space
- Placing one on your chest and the other hand under your ribcage
- Tune in to see what your current breathing pattern is, and also what type or length of breaths you're taking
- Readjust your breathing if you feel out of sync (to fast/shallow/short etc.) or continue your breath rate if it feels comfortable and natural.

**4-2-4 Equal Breathing:**

- Inhale deeply for 4 counts.
- Hold for 2 counts,
- Exhale for 4 counts.
- Repeat

**Box or 4 Count Breathing:**

- Inhale for 4 counts
- Hold for 4 counts
- Exhale for 4 counts
- Hold for 4 counts
- Repeat

**4-2-6 Breathing**

- Inhale deeply and slowly count to 4, expanding your belly as you do so,
- Hold that breath for a count of 2,
- Slowly exhale though your mouth for a count of 6,
- Repeat

**4-7-8 Breathing Technique**

- Inhale deeply and slowly count to 4, expanding your belly as you do so,
- Hold that breath for a count of 7,
- Slowly exhale though your mouth for a count of 8,
- Repeat for a few minutes.

**Alternate Nostril Breathing:**

- Hold the right thumb over the right nostril and inhale deeply through the left nostril. (If that feels unsafe - partially block the right nostril instead of closing it off completely)
- At the peak of inhalation, close off the left nostril using your other thumb, then exhale through the open right nostril.
- Continue this alternation and/ or swap starting nostril.

**"Voo" Breathing:**

- Notice your breath before you start for 20 seconds
- Take a deep slow breath in through your nose
- Breathe out through your mouth making an audible "Voo" foghorn sound.
- Repeat the breaths in and "Voo" exhales for as long as you desire or for 3-5mins.

*For additional breathing exercises you can take specific breathwork classes in person or online. There are also several free classes available on the internet. Just ensure you check with you doctor before attempting breathwork.*

# GENERAL SELF CARE

......................................

- Making sure your basic needs are met

- Getting as much sleep as you can

- Nourishing food and daily water intake met

- Making sure your environment is free of as much clutter/mess to help Executive Functioning and sensory stimulation. (Also making your environment a happy, cosy, safe space that matches your needs and/or Human Design)

- Daily or as-needed Body Scan Activity

- Resting on the couch or in your bed as needed

- Listening to your body - no guilt around resting. For those who are way out of alignment/burnt out/in a Freeze (Dorsal) dominate state- you will need more rest than you think you do.)

- Adding More Neuroceptive Safety Signs

- Reducing/Removing Neurocepetive Danger Signs

- Setting Up Home & Work to aid "hack" your Executive Functioning

- Vagus Nerve Exercises (See page 146)

- Epsom Salt foot soaks or baths

- Heat Packs on areas of tension while reading/watching TV/relaxing /meditation etc.

- Using Ice Packs on your chest while reading/watching TV/relaxing /meditation etc.

- Power pose and intuitive stretching before bed/in the morning

- Self-Massages – gentle pressure on trigger points using moisturiser or magnesium spray

- Dry Body Brushing before shower/bath

- Acupressure mats before bedtime

- Weighted blankets while reading/ winding down for bed

- Using essential oils/diffusing in your home or safe spaces

- Gratitude Reflections – whether written in a journal or if journals are Danger Sign from childhood experiences, you can say them aloud or in your head, say them in the car or shower etc.

- Mindful creative activities: working with clay, painting, embroidery, knitting, crocheting, colouring in

- Affirmations: You can use "What if" instead or "I am" to help with any disconnect you may consciously or unconsciously have (See Affirmation list)

Rituals are simple
steps or routines
infused with
intention, meaning,
and presence that can
bring you back into
Alignment.

———

EVA HATTIN

# TEN

........................................

# RITUALS

## 'BOTTOM UP'
## RESOURCES & STRATEGIES

Rituals provide a sense of luxury, safety, and stability in our often chaotic worlds. They help to ground us in the moment and act as moments of consistent, mindful self-care.

As we go through our days, we can unintentionally take on other people's energy or don't fully process our emotions and experiences for whatever reason. The body keeps score and all our unprocessed emotions can begin to take their toll on our Nervous Systems over time.

Getting into the habit of creating small moments throughout our week to engage with these rituals has far more benefits than a large one-off self-care moment. These small moments each day can help discharge all the extra energetic 'baggage' you may have picked up during the day.

The following section contains examples of simple daily rituals or little luxuries you can use to help signal a sense of safety to your Nervous System and return your state of flow after any daily stressors.

# VAGUS NERVE EXERCISES

..................................

**EXERCISE DISCLAIMER:**

Before you attempt any of these exercises, please consult with your doctor.

The following exercises come from and are adapted/inspired by the research of Steven Porges & Stanley Rosenberg and incorporates the concepts of crossing the midline & bilateral eye movements. These Vagus Nerve exercises can help keep your Autonomic Nervous System healthy and functioning optimally. They also provide some calming Parasympathetic energy. They can be done as needed throughout the day and week or when you feel the intuitive nudge.

# VAGUS NERVE
# EXERCISE ONE

..................................

**Purpose:**

To gently reposition your neck to increase mobility in your neck and spine. In doing so it enables more blood to flow to the brainstem and the corresponding cranial nerves that are used for our Aligned Ventral Vagal, rest and digest, state.

**Before you begin:**

Bring some awareness to your neck's range of movement. Rotate your head to the left and right and see how much resistance or stiffness is present. Lie down in a comfortable space.

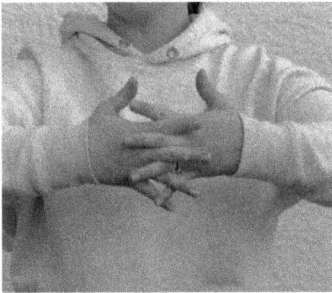

**01**    Bring your hands together in front of you and interlock your fingers together.

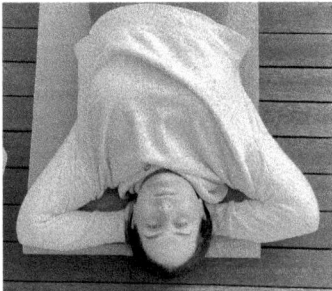

**02**    Keeping your fingers interlocked, reach over your head; raise your head slightly; and place your hands behind your head. The weight of your head should be resting comfortably in the palms of your hands.

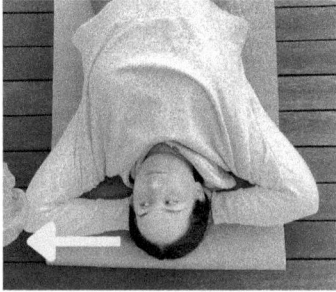

$O3$ Keep your head and arms in this position. Without moving your head, look to the left as far as you can without straining or causing discomfort. Hold this position.

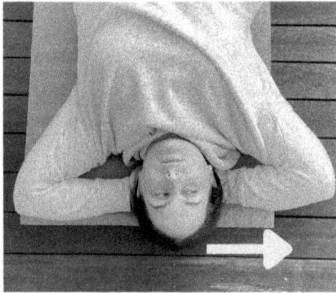

$O4$ Depending on your nervous system's state, you may feel the need to take a deep breath/yawn/swallow/sigh anywhere from a few seconds - up to a minute in. Keeping your head and hands in the same position, shift your gaze to the right and repeat Step 3.

**After:**

Rotate your head to the left and right. Notice the change in your neck's range of movement and compare it to the resistance or stiffness you felt before. You may feel incredibly relaxed and possibly drowsy after this exercise.

# VAGUS NERVE EXERCISE TWO

......................................

**Purpose:**
To gently reduce forward head pressure, improve spine alignment, release tension in your upper back/spine, and allow more space in your upper chest for optimal breathing.

**Before you begin:**
Sit or stand in a comfortable position.

## 01
Keeping your head facing forwards, look to the right.

## 02
While holding this right gaze, slowly tilt your head to the right. The right side of your face should be moving towards your right shoulder. Stop when you feel tension or discomfort. Hold this position for up to a minute or until you take a deep breath, yawn, swallow or sigh.

03

Slowly move your head up so that it returns to its neutral position & return your gaze to forward facing.
Look to the left.

04

While holding this left gaze, slowly tilt your head to the left. The left side of your face should be moving towards your left shoulder. Stop when you feel tension or discomfort. Hold this position for up to a minute or until you take a deep breath, yawn, swallow or sigh.

**After:**

Slowly move your head up so that it returns to its neutral position & return your gaze to forward facing.

# VAGUS NERVE
# EXERCISE THREE

·····························

**Purpose:**
To gently reduce forward head pressure, improve spine alignment, release tension in your upper back/spine, and allow more space in your upper chest for optimal breathing.

**Before you begin:**
Sit or stand in a comfortable position.

O1    Keeping your head facing forwards, look to the right.

O2    While holding this right gaze, slowly tilt your head to the left. The left side of your face should be moving towards your left shoulder. Stop when you feel tension or discomfort. Hold this position for up to a minute or until you take a deep breath, yawn, swallow or sigh. You can use your hand to help hold the stretch.

03 Slowly move your head up so that it returns to its neutral position & return your gaze to forward facing.
Look to the left.

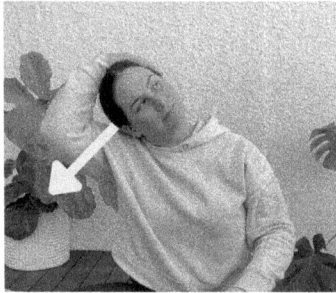

04 While holding this left gaze, slowly tilt your head to the right. The left side of your face should be moving towards your right shoulder. Stop when you feel tension or discomfort. Hold this position for up to a minute or until you take a deep breath, yawn, swallow or sigh. You can use your hand to help hold the stretch.

**After:**

Slowly move your head up so that it returns to its neutral position & return your gaze to forward facing.

# VAGUS NERVE EXERCISE FOUR
## -EAR MASSAGE-

........................................

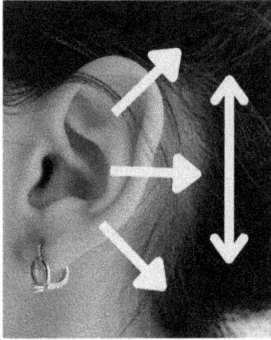

**01** Gently pull the outer part of your left ear away from your skull. Wiggle your ear up and down. Bring your awareness to any resistance you feel/notice when moving your ear around. Is the tension in one direction only?

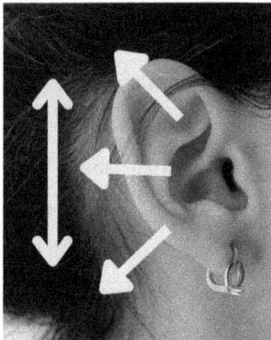

**02** Repeat step one with the right ear. Compare what your right ear feels like compared to your left ear. Does one side hold more tension? Or do they feel the same?

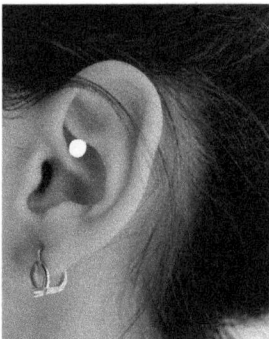

**03** Locate the acupressure point situated in the hollow/section just above your right ear canal. Using your index finger, using very little pressure, rotate your finger on the acupressure point. You can gently massage this pressure point for as long as you feel like it.
You may feel the need to take a deep breath, sigh, yawn or swallow.

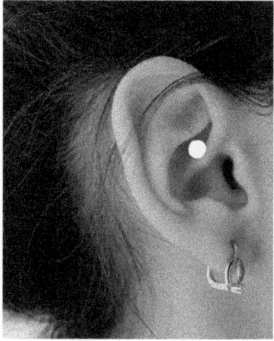

04     Repeat Step 3 on your left ear.

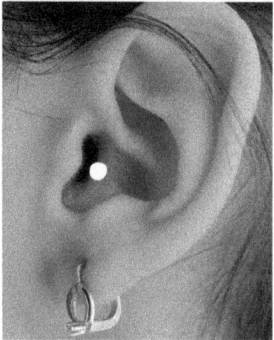

05     Locate the acupressure point situated at the entrance to your right ear canal; it is on the side closest to the back of your head. Using your index finger, using very little pressure, rotate your finger on the acupressure point. You can gently massage this pressure point for as long as you feel like it. You may feel the need to take a deep breath, sigh, yawn or swallow.

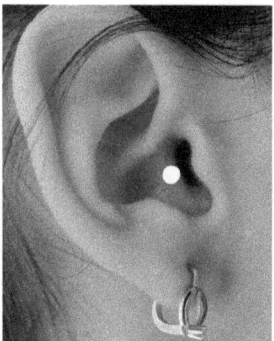

06     Repeat Step 5 with your left ear.

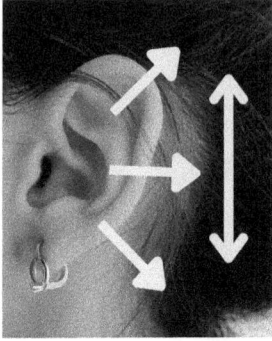

07    Repeat Step 1 and 2 again.

# VAGUS NERVE EXERCISE FIVE
## -FACE MASSAGE-

..................................

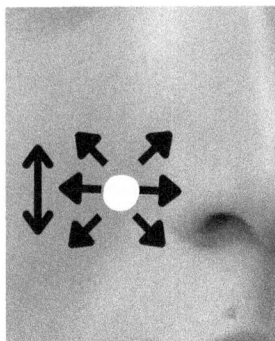

**01** Using light pressure, place your finger on the acupressure point on your right-hand side.

**02** Slowly and gently wiggle your finger around in circles and up and down, left and right, in diagonal movements, bringing awareness to any feeling of resistance.

**03** If you notice any directional resistance, lean into that resistance by lightly pushing in that direction, holding, and allowing it to release.
You may take a deep breath, yawn, sigh or swallow at this point.

**04** Repeat Steps 1-3 again with a little more pressure to access the deeper facial muscle layers.

**05** Repeat Steps 1-3 again with a firm pressure to access the deepest facial muscle layers and connective tissue- it should feel like you are comfortably pressing on the bone.

# VAGUS NERVE EXERCISE FIVE
## -FACE MASSAGE-

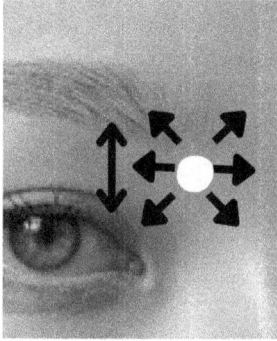

......................................

**06** Using light pressure, place your finger on the acupressure point on your right-hand side.

**07** Slowly and gently wiggle your finger/thumb around in circles and up and down, left and right, in diagonal movements, bringing awareness to any feeling of resistance.

**08** If you notice any directional resistance, lean into that resistance by lightly pushing in that direction, holding, and allowing it to release.
You may take a deep breath, yawn, sigh or swallow at this point.

**09** Repeat Steps 7-8 again with a little more pressure to access the deeper facial muscle layers.

**10** Repeat Steps 7-8 again with a firm pressure to access the deepest facial muscle layers and connective tissue- it should feel like you are comfortably pressing on the bone.

**11** Repeat Steps 1- 10 again on the left-hand side of your face.

# ACCUPRESSURE POINTS ASSOCIATED WITH THE VAGUS NERVE

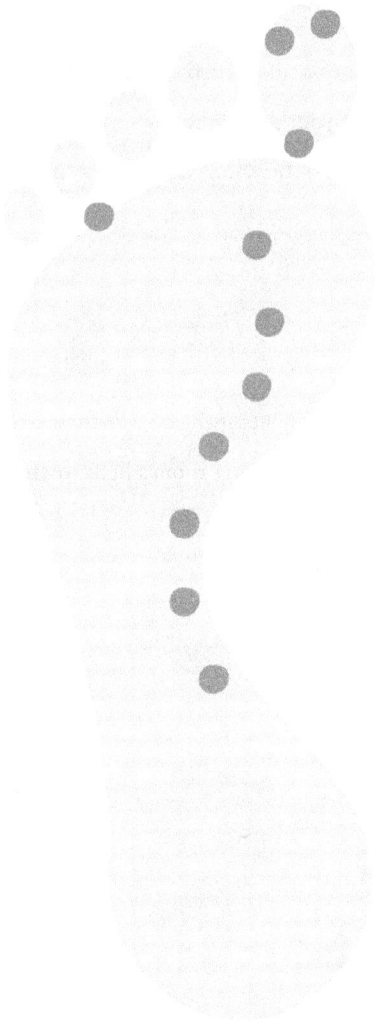

..........................................

Right Underside        Left Underside

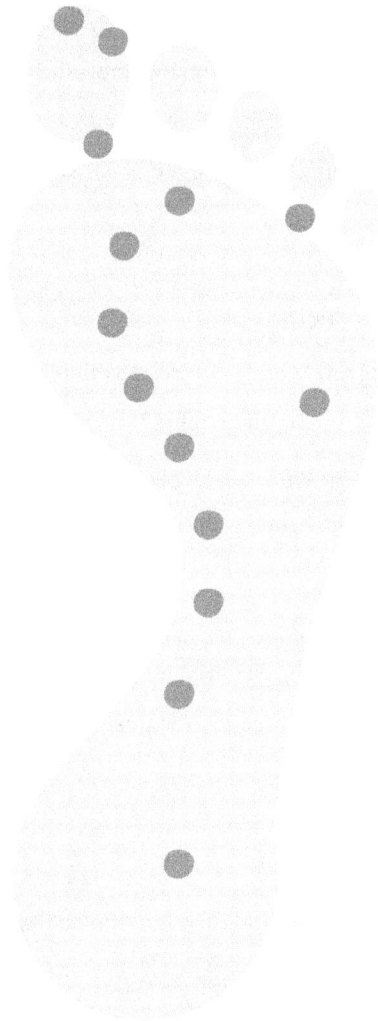

# 5MIN DRY BODY
# BRUSHING RITUAL

••••••••••••••••••••••••••••••••

**BEFORE YOU BEGIN:**

- For maximum benefits, complete the ritual right before your evening shower or bath when your skin is completely dry
- Use gentle, comfortable strokes with light pressure to stimulate the skin, not scratch it
- Avoid inflamed, broken, and/or sensitive parts of your skin and body
- Your skin may show some signs of redness after brushing due to the increased circulation

**LIGHTING:**

Using soft lighting can create a calm & cosy atmosphere

- A sunset lamp; a plug-in nightlight; a candle; the soft light setting on a diffuser etc.
- Turning off the main bathroom light & using the adjoining room's light to create a softer lighting atmosphere

**SCENT:**

- Diffusing essential oils
- Burning Sage, Palo Santo, incense or a scented candle

**SOUND:**

- Silence
- Calming music or white/brown noise etc.

# 5MIN DRY BODY
# BRUSHING RITUAL

...............................

01  Starting at your right foot and ankle, brush towards the heart in
    long rhythmic strokes.
    Swap to the left foot and ankle and repeat.

02  Slowly move up your body. Continuing the long rhythmic strokes
    from your left ankle to the top of your thighs and buttocks. Be sure to
    use very light strokes under your knees and avoid your pelvic region.
    Swap to your right side and repeat.

03  Move your focus to your arms. Starting with your right hand, brush towards
    your elbows in long rhythmic strokes.
    Then move the strokes from your elbows to your shoulders.
    Be sure to use very light strokes under your armpits.
    Swap to your left hand and repeat

04  Using gentle circular movements, brush your chest, stomach, back and
    shoulders. Avoid brushing breasts, neck and face as the skin and these areas
    are very sensitive/delicate.

05  Shower as usual and apply body oil or moisturiser of your choice.

ADDITIONAL RITUALS:
- *Shower Ritual*
- *Vagus Nerve Facial Massage*

# NIGHTLY SHOWER
# RITUAL

..................................

**BEFORE YOU BEGIN:**

Additional Ritual: *Dry Body Brushing Ritual to stimulate skin*

**LIGHTING:**

Using soft lighting can create a calm & cosy atmosphere

- A sunset lamp; a plug-in nightlight; a candle; the soft light setting on a diffuser etc.
- Turning off the main bathroom light & using the adjoining room's light to create a softer lighting atmosphere

**SCENT:**

- Diffusing essential oils
- Using an essential oil shower bomb/diffuser steamer tablet/ shower mist
- Hanging fresh eucalyptus leaves over the shower head
- Burning Sage, Palo Santo, incense or a scented candle

**SOUND:**

- Silence
- Calming music or white/brown noise etc.

**GATHER:**

- Body oil/lotion/Magnesium Spray, cleansing cloth/exfoliating towel, cosy bath towel, robe, cosy clothes, hair, body & face products etc.

**DRINK:**

- Iced water & lemon/cucumber for after the shower

# NIGHTLY SHOWER
# RITUAL

....................................

**01**  Prepare your calm, grounding shower environment by diffusing essential oils; spraying the shower mist or adding a shower steamer/eucalyptus branch to the shower; turn on the soft warm lighting; gather all your body and facial products; set out your post-shower clothes/robe/slippers etc. *(Additional Body Brushing Ritual)*

**02**  While the water is heating up, close your eyes (if it feels safe to do so), place one hand on your chest and the other hand on your stomach and take three slow deep breaths (can be done standing still or swaying from side to side if that feels safer).

**03**  Cleanse face, body & hair. Exfoliate

**04**  Step out; dry off; apply body oil/lotion/Magnesium Spray & face products. *(Additional Ritual: Vagus Nerve Facial Massage using face products).*

**05**  Put on comfortable clothes & enjoy post shower drink.
You can then use a heat pack or Shakti Mat while you relax in bed.

# EPSOM/MAGNESIUM SALT SOAK RITUAL

........................................

**BEFORE YOU BEGIN:**

Additional Ritual: *Dry Body Brushing Ritual to stimulate skin*

**LIGHTING:**

Using soft lighting can create a calm & cosy atmosphere

- A sunset lamp; a plug-in nightlight; a candle; the soft light setting on a diffuser etc.
- Turning off the main bathroom light & using the adjoining room's light to create a softer lighting atmosphere

**SCENT:**

- Diffusing essential oils
- Using an essential oil shower bomb/diffuser steamer tablet/ shower mist
- Hanging fresh eucalyptus leaves over the shower head
- Burning Sage, Palo Santo, incense or a scented candle

**SOUND:**

- Silence
- Calming music or white/brown noise etc.

**GATHER:**

- Body oil/lotion/Magnesium Spray, cleansing cloth/exfoliating towel, cosy bath towel, robe, cosy clothes, hair, body & face products etc.
- A book, podcast, meditation or magazine etc.

**DRINK:**

- Iced water & lemon/cucumber for after the soak

# EPSOM/MAGNESIUM SALT SOAK RITUAL

· · · · · · · · · · · · · · · · · · · · · · · · · · · ·

**01** Prepare your calm, grounding shower environment by diffusing essential oils; spraying the shower mist or adding a eucalyptus branch to the bath tap; turn on the soft warm lighting; gather all your body and facial products; set out your post-shower clothes/robe/slippers etc.
*(Additional Body Brushing Ritual)*

**02** Turn the bath on, and add Epsom salts to water. While the bath is filling up, close your eyes (if it feels safe to do so), place one hand on your chest and the other hand on your stomach and take three slow deep breaths (standing still or swaying from side to side if that feels safer)

**03** Soak in the tub for as long as you like while your body is restoring your magnesium levels & relieving muscle tension. You could do some breathing exercises; listen to a meditation, or read a book.

**04** Step out; dry off; apply body oil/lotion & face products.
*(Additional Ritual: Vagus Nerve Facial Massage using face products).*

**05** Put on comfortable clothes & enjoy post shower drink.
You can then use a heat pack or Shakti Mat while you relax in bed.

# VAGUS NERVE FACIAL
# MASSAGE RITUAL

·····································

**BEFORE YOU BEGIN:**

Additional Ritual: *Dry Body Brushing Ritual to stimulate skin or Shower Ritual*

**LIGHTING:**

Using soft lighting can create a calm & cosy atmosphere

- A sunset lamp; a plug-in nightlight; a candle; the soft light setting on a diffuser etc.
- Turning off the main bathroom light & using the adjoining room's light to create a softer lighting atmosphere

**SCENT:**

- Diffusing essential oils
- Burning Sage, Palo Santo, incense or a scented candle

**SOUND:**

- Silence
- Calming music or white/brown noise etc.

**GATHER:**

- Facial oils, serums, moisturiser, facial treatments etc.

**DRINK:**

- Iced water & lemon/cucumber for after the soak

# VAGUS NERVE FACIAL
# MASSAGE RITUAL

...............................

01   Pump Facial product/s into your hands. If products contain a calming scent, cup hands and inhale deeply a few times. Otherwise, Take a few deep slow breaths. Apply facial products all over your face and neck.

02   Starting at your right collarbone, perform continuous upwards strokes, stopping when you reach your jaw. Work your way across your neck, ending at your left collarbone.

03   Rub products all over your face again. Using light pressure, find and place your finger on the acupressure points next to your nose.

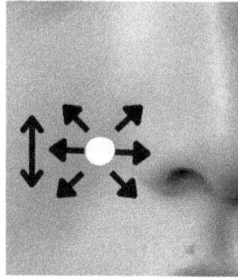

04   Slowly and gently wiggle your fingers around in circles and up and down, left and right, in diagonal movements, bringing awareness to any feeling of resistance. If you notice any directional resistance, lean into that resistance by lightly pushing in that direction, holding, and allowing it to release. You may take a deep breath, yawn, sigh or swallow at this point.

05   Move towards your earlobes now. Using both hands, place two fingers behind your earlobes. Slowly and gently rotate your fingers in little circles.

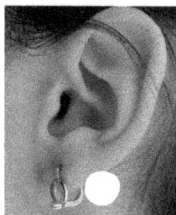

# VAGUS NERVE FACIAL
# MASSAGE RITUAL

..................................

**06** Wash your hands to remove products if you do not want any of the facial products in your hair.

**07** Interlock your fingers/hands in front of you. Move your hands over your head and rest them/palms of your hands on the back of your head.

**08** Keep your head and arms in this position. Without moving your head, look to the left as far as you can without straining or causing discomfort. Hold this position.

**09** Depending on your nervous system's state, you will feel the need to take a deep breath, yawn, swallow or sigh anywhere from a few seconds up to a minute. Keeping your head and hands in the same position, shift your gaze to the right and hold. Return your gaze to the centre. Take one last deep breath.

**10** Move both of your arms down by your sides. Roll your shoulders backwards three times and then roll them forwards three times.

# BEDTIME RELAXATION RITUAL

......................................

**BEFORE YOU BEGIN:**

Additional Ritual: *Dry Body Brushing Ritual to stimulate skin, Shower or Epsom Salt Soak Ritual, and/or Vagus Nerve Facial Massage Ritual*

**LIGHTING:**

Using soft lighting can create a calm & cosy atmosphere

- A sunset lamp; a plug-in nightlight; a candle; the soft light setting on a diffuser etc.
- No lighting if desired

**SCENT:**

- Diffusing essential oils
- Lavender room or pillow mist

**SOUND:**

- Silence
- Calming music or white/brown noise etc

**GATHER:**

- Heat Pack or Ice Pack, Eye Mask/Lavender Eye Pack, Shakti Mat, weighted blanket, Lavender Spray,
- Additional pillows
- Glass of water

# BEDTIME RELAXATION
# RITUAL

...................................

01  Spray your room/bed/pillow with Lavender spray or a calming essential oil blend. If using, place your Shakti Mat onto your bed.

02  Hop into bed. Place a pillow under your knees to increase comfort and take a sip of water.

03  Place the heat pack in areas of tension or wrap it around your shoulders or place the ice pack, wrapped in a cloth/tea towel, onto your chest/décolletage. If using, place weighted blanket on chest/stomach and/or place the eye pack/mask over eyes. Adjust or remove these as needed.

04  Place one hand on chest and the other hand on stomach. Become a gentle observer by bringing awareness to your breathing rate and the sensations in your body.

05  You can either take full slow breaths while you take some time to relax or you could use any of the grounding breathing exercises found in this book

06  Once you feel drowsy or calmer, remove items and fall asleep/continue your night-time routine.

# CACAO/HOT BEVERAGE
# GRATITUDE RITUAL

••••••••••••••••••••••••••••••••

**BEFORE YOU BEGIN:**

Make your beverage & find a calm comfortable spot to journal and reflect in.

Possible locations: your bed, outdoor settings, in the bath, your workspace etc.

**GATHER:**

- Cacao/Hot Beverage;
- Journal & Pen
- Candle
- Essential Oils, Sage or Palo Santo
- Oracle Cards and/or Tarot Cards

01    Sit in a comfortable position. Close your eyes if it feels safe to do so. Take several deep slow breaths. You can sit still or if that feels uncomfortable, you can slowly sway from side to side.

02    Slowly and mindfully sip your hot drink, while journaling, reflecting and/or setting intentions.

03    Once you have finished drinking your hot beverage, you may feel called to meditate or stretch intuitively.
This is also a great time to complete a few Vagus Nerve exercises.

# MY SMUDGING/SAGING RITUAL

••••••••••••••••••••••••••••••

**BEFORE YOU BEGIN:**

Open Doors & Windows in home.

**GATHER:**

- Palo Santo or Sage,
- Lighter or matches
- Fireproof bowl

01    Begin at your house's front entry way. Hold Palo Santo over the bowl to catch the ashes. Set an intention to purify and remove negative energy and blockages. Light the Palo Santo. Wait till the Palo Santo begins to smoulder or using your hand, wave over the Palo Santo to extinguish the flame.

02    Close your eyes, if it feels safe to do so, and slowly wave the smoke over yourself, around your head, arms, legs etc. Be mindful of the ashes as the Palo Santo smoulders.

03    While holding your cleansing intention, walk in a clockwise movement around your home while fanning the smoke into every corner of each of the rooms & spaces you cleanse.

04    Once you have finished, Let the Palo Santo burn out in the fireproof bowl and return the ashes to the earth. Monitor it to reduce any fire hazard risk.

# ESSENTIAL OILS

....................................

The Olfactory System is responsible for our sense of smell. Once a scent has been detected by our nose, the nerves send information/signals about that particular scent to our brain. The information about the scent can then conjure up specific memories as well as provide information to our bodies than can influence our emotions, mood, and behaviour. Having or using a specific scent can then become a safety signal for your nervous system to help move your back into alignment/regulation when ever your feel low frequency/dysregulated.

Here are several lists of essential oils and the properties. You can diffuse a single oil or create a unique combination. You can also use them to create a personal perfume or body oil by mixing them with a carrier oil.

Alternatively you can use familiar scents to you; the smell of coffee, the ocean, a specific flower ect.

| Energising Oils | Grounding Oils | Calming oils |
|---|---|---|
| Grapefruit | Palo Santo | **Laven**der |
| Pineapple Sage | White Sage | Ylang Ylang |
| Lemon | Sandalwood | Clary Sage |
| Lemon Myrtle | Patchouli | Eucalyptus |
| Lime | Ylang Ylang | Spearmint |
| Mint | Ginger | Lemongrass |
| Spearmint | Basil | Frankincense |
| Peppermint | Geranium | Geranium |
| White Fir | Vetiver | Jasmine |
| Orange | Frankincense | Juniper Berry |
| Tangerine | Rose | Chamomile |
| Bergamot | | Vetiver |

# VAGUS NERVE
# ESSENTIAL OIL BLENDS

••••••••••••••••••••••••••••••

**Carrier Oil:** Jojoba
**Essential Oils:** Bergamot, Lavender, Ylang Ylang, Orange, Geranium, Patchouli


**Carrier Oil:** Jojoba
**Essential Oils:** Lavender, Bergamot, Ylang Ylang


**Carrier Oil:** Jojoba
**Essential Oils:** Lemon-Scented Tea-Tree, Juniper, Lavender, Rosemary, Lime, Roman Chamomile


**Carrier Oil:** Jojoba
**Essential Oils:** Frankincense, Roman Chamomile, Peppermint, Juniper, Copaiba, Helichrysum

With every act of self-care your authentic self gets stronger, and the critical, fearful mind gets weaker. Every act of self-care is a powerful declaration: I am on my side, I am on my side, each day I am more and more on my own side.

———

SUSAN WEISS BERRY

# ELEVEN

........................................

# HOW TO IMPLIMENT ALL
# THIS INFORMATION
## -THE SELF CARE PLAN-

My first thought after collecting and collating everything I knew about the Autonomic Nervous System was... How do I bring this all together and implement this?

As I stared at the notes spread across my dining table, I thought back to my classroom days and how I would break down concepts and topics into learning stages. So I went about making a plan and laying out implementation stages for me to follow.

Now, this example self-care plan is based on my needs and learning style. You have the option of following my implementation stage suggestions or you can adapt it to suit your needs and wants. My only non-negotiable is Stage One. You need to consult your health practitioner.

Each implementation stage's time length will vary, for some people it may be a few days to weeks to work through a stage. Others may be working through a stage for several months. It doesn't matter. Take your time. Remember, you need to ensure your Nervous System feels safe and rushing through and overwhelming yourself with tasks can have the opposite desired effect.

As life and our Nervous Systems States are ever-evolving, it's best to check in with your plans once a week/month to reevaluate. If having a set routine for what day you will implement certain strategies, resources, and rituals appeals to you, you can create a weekly or monthly plan. If that isn't your style or part of your Human Design, you can refer back to the resources and intuitively choose based on your current needs or wants.

# STAGE ONE
Consultation

Before you begin to create and implement your Self-Care Plan, make sure you have consulted with your healthcare providers. Non-Negotiable is your General Physician/Doctor First.

**Highlight or select other professionals from the lists:**

## Specialised/Licenced Support Options:

- Acupuncture
- Allergy and Immunology -
- Chiropractor
- Craniosacral Therapy
- Dietician
- Doctor/GP
- Domestic Violence/Abuse hotlines and community support networks
- Doula / Postpartum Doula
- Greif & Loss Hotline and community support networks
- HeartMath - heartmath.org
- Hydrotherapy
- Kinesiologist

- Lactation & Breastfeeding Consultants
- Massage Therapist
- Mental Health Hotlines & community services
- Naturopath
- OBGYN
- Occupational Therapist
- Optometrist
- Physiotherapist
- Reflexology
- Therapist, Psychologist etc.
- Sensory Deprivation Pods
- Sleep Study

**Alternative Therapies Options:**

- Aura Cleansing
- Binaural beats
- Breathwork
- Brown Noise
- Burning incense
- Chakra Cleanse
- Charging & working with crystals
- Chinese Medicine
- Cleansing space with salt
- Clearing clutter & airing out home
- EFT Tapping - Emotional Freedom Techniques
- Energy Clearing/Cleansing
- Equine-assisted Therapy (Horses)

- Essential oils
- Grounding
- Hydrotherapy
- Hypnotherapy
- Neurolinguistic Programming
- Reiki
- Sacred Medicine
- Smudging or Saging
- Sound baths
- Therapy Dog or Animal
- Timeline therapy & Akashic Records
- White Noise

**Notes:**

# STAGE TWO
Nervous System Awareness & Identification

Tasks:

- Complete the Basic Needs Reflection Tool on page 103. Identify areas where you can possibly implement small changes to ensure as many of your basic needs can be met daily, weekly etc.

- Rest

- If you haven't already, create your Personal Nervous System Blueprint on page 45. This will help you map out your Nervous System States and their associated actions, thoughts, emotions, and mental stories.

- Determine your current baseline state. You can refer back to your Personal Nervous System. Knowing roughly what your baseline state is will help you determine what regulation and self-care strategies will best support you.

    *What State do you currently resonate with? Aligned/Fight/Flight/Freeze?*
    *Are you mainly Regulated and dipping in and out of Fight/Flight?*
    *Are you mainly living in Fight/Flight and dipping in and out of Freeze?*
    *Are you mainly living in Freeze?*

- Choose 1-3 main default regulation responses you can fall back on when you become aware you're entering into or are already in a Survival Stress Response. Make sure you feel comfortable with them. The goal is to stay within your Window of Tolerance/ help you to feel safe while conducting them.
    *(See following page for choices)*

## When I am in my Out of Alignment, Fight/Flight Stress Response, these are my main regulation strategies:

- Rubbing hands/body vigorously
- Extending spine to correct posture
- Physical contact
- "Voo" Breathing
- Grounding exercises
- Slow full even breaths
- Humming
- Centring exercise
- Shaking or moving body
- Rocking/swaying
- Bringing awareness to my feets contact points
- Deep Pressure
- Dancing
- Laughing
- Creative Activities

## When I am in my Out of Alignment, Freeze Stress Response, these are my main regulation strategies:

- Calling "Safety Sign" Person
- Visualising "Safety Sign" Person
- Grounding exercises
- Body Scan
- Bringing awareness to my body while walking
- Sensory Defences - adding or taking away sensory stimuli
- Taking a few short sharp inhales then taking some full deep breaths
- Sleep/Rest
- Deep pressure
- Adding more pressure to contact points of feet - digging feet into the ground
- Using "Safety Sign" Scent

Also...

- In both responses, I can remove myself from the situation so that I can to take a moment to regulate myself.

- **Try implementing one or two of the Deep Breathing & Vagus Nerve Exercises.** Make sure you have consulted with your healthcare practitioner before attempting the Breathing or Vagus Nerve exercises, Take it slow. If anything causes physical or emotional discomfort, discontinue and consult your healthcare provider.

# STAGE THREE
Awareness & Identification of Safety & Danger Signs:

**Tasks:**

- If you haven't already, identify your personal Safety and Danger Signs on page 29.
- Work your way through the Limiting Belief Reflection Tool and reflective question prompts on page 108.

**Continue:**

- Basic Needs: Continue to implement small changes to ensure as many of your basic needs can be met daily, weekly etc.

- -Continue to rest.

- Awareness of States & Implement Regulation Strategies: Try to bring awareness to what Nervous System state you are currently in. If you notice you are in a Survival Stress Response, use one of your pre-selected regulation strategies to harness some mobilising or calming energy.

- Continue with some Breathing and Vagus Nerve Exercises throughout the week.

# STAGE FOUR
Setting up your environment for success


It's time to start setting up your environment for success based on your identified personal Safety and Danger Signs as well as your Human Design Environment Archetype. This is also the time that we will begin creating an environment that nurtures and takes a bit of pressure off your Executive Functioning ability. This section may take more time than expected. Try not to rush or force this process.

**Tasks:**

Remove or reduce any items that are associated with Danger Signs by:

- Declutter, Donate, Recycle, Put into storage etc.
- Find a home for every item you have and organise those spaces.
- Deep Clean or hire a cleaner to do a bond clean.
- Source, find or purchase any items that help you to feel safe, gives you a sign of Safety, make you feel calm and happy etc. as well as anything that will assist in your executive functioning & organisation.
- Reorganise your wardrobe so that you can create a capsule wardrobe with your Safety Sign clothing and jewellery etc.
- Cleaning out your bag/ purse/car/garden/porch/phone/email inbox/ social media etc.

**What other ways or things can you think of that can help to set your environment up for success?**

Specific diffusing scents, creating a better sleep environment, certain strategies from the executive functioning sections etc.

**Notes:**

**Continue:**

- Basic Needs: Continue to implement small changes to ensure as many of your basic needs can be met daily, weekly etc.

- Awareness of States & Implement Regulation Strategies: Try to bring awareness to what Nervous System state you are currently in. If you notice you are in a Survival Stress Response, use one of your pre-selected regulation strategies to harness some mobilising or calming energy.

- Continue with some Breathing and Vagus Nerve Exercises throughout the week.

- Keep adding Safety Signs to your environment

- Keep identifying, reducing or removing Danger Signs from your environment

# STAGE FIVE
Self-Care Strategies, Rituals & Routines for success

Brainstorm and identify strategies, rituals and routines to nurture your Nervous System and Executive Functioning skills. Select strategies and resources from following sections:

Using threes separate colours, work though the support options and colour code them to show:

- Things I am already doing that I will bring more awareness too
- Things that I would like to slowly begin to implement each day/week/month
- Things that I would like to implement later on so that I don't overwhelm my Nervous System

## Vagus Nerve Support:

- Vagal Exercise One
- Vagal Exercise Two
- Vagal Exercise Three
- Vagal Exercise Four Ear Massage
- Vagal Exercise Five Facial Massage
- Breathing Exercises
- Nutrition
- Lying on right side
- Loud Humming/Singing
- Correct Posture & aligning spine

- Self Relaxation Massage
- Professional Massage
- Foot Massage-Reflexology
- Social Connection
- Coregulation with others
- Cold Exposure
- Gargling Excessively
- Consciously Gagging
- Bilateral Eye Movements

## Strategies, Rituals & Routines for success:

- Somatic Exercises
- Progressive Muscle Relaxation
- Acupressure Mats
- Deep Pressure-Hugs/Wall Push
- Yoga
- Tai Chi
- Pilates

- Gentle Walking
- Intuitive Stretching
- Grounding Exercises
- Holding a Yoga pose for 1min
- Balance Exercises

**Sleep Support:**

- Nap when possible
- Using Sleep Calculator
- Safe sun exposure during day
- Set your bed up for success
- Set you room up for success

- Bedtime/winddown routine
- Limit Screen time before bed
- Limit exercise before bed
- Vagus Exercises before bed

**Self Care & Rituals::**

- Interoception – Body Scan
- Resting - listening to body
- Meditation
- Yoga Pose/Stretch before bed
- Affirmations
- Essential Oils/Magnesium Spray
- Face Massage Ritual
- Gratitude Ritual
- Shower Ritual
- Cacao/Drink Ritual
- Dry Body Brushing

- Bedtime Ritual
- Heat packs before bed
- Acupressure mats
- Weighted Blankets
- Icepacks on Chest
- Mindful Creative Activities
- Baths/ Epsom Salt Soaks
- Foot Baths
- Self Massages

**Mindful Activities:**

- Gratitude
- Clay
- Process Art
- Painting
- Drawing
- Colouring in
- Stretching/Breathing Exercises
- Listening to rain sounds
- Cacao/Hot Chocolates
- Cloud/Sky Gazing
- Gardening
- Watching ocean/firepit
- At home facial

- Knitting/Sewing/Embroidery
- Slow walks
- Easy Bike Rides
- Yoga/Pilates
- Sound Baths
- Baths/Soaks
- Massages
- Reading
- Watching Comedies
- Hair Masks
- Meditation
- Cooking/Baking

**Continue:**

- Basic Needs: Continue to implement small changes to ensure as many of your basic needs can be met daily, weekly etc.

- Awareness of States & Implement Regulation Strategies: Try to bring awareness to what nervous system state you are currently in. If you notice you are in a Survival Stress Response, use one of your pre-selected regulation strategies to harness some mobilising or calming energy.

- Continue with some Breathing and Vagus Nerve Exercises throughout the week.

- Continue to rest.

- Keep adding Safety Signs to your environment.

- Keep identifying, reducing or removing Danger Signs from your environment.

- Keep implementing your selected Self-Care Strategies, Rituals & Routines for success

# After a few weeks to months

- Start from the Stage One again and revisit each stage again to review or update any changes. Your needs and your Nervous System's needs are ever evolving so it is good to check in every so often.

# THANK YOU
# & FINAL THOUGHTS

First off, I want to thank you for trusting and coming on this healing journey with me. I know it was a lot of new information to process. One thing I have learned over the past five years or so is that having a strong and healthy Nervous System sets the foundations for and breeds abundance. Sure, there will be times when things happen and you are pushed Out-of-Alignment but now you have the knowledge and resources you can use to help soothe your Nervous System and move back into Flow.

No more living in and attracting things from a low vibrational stress state.

Seeing as we have now primed your Nervous System and Reticular Activating System for abundance and built a strong foundation for Manifestation, I would highly recommend looking into experienced coaches and guides who can assist you to incorporate some "Level One & Up" strategies and Top-Down mindset work seeing as my zone of genius is Emotional Intelligence and Nervous System Regulation. I have included some additional reading and resource suggestions in the following sections but encourage you to use your intuition when selecting coaches and programs to work with. Double check that both you and your Nervous System feel safe with the coach or program before signing up... make it an intuitive holistically aligned purchase and not a purchase from a dysregulated Fight, Flight, Freeze state.

Remember, your success is inevitable!

Lots of love,
- Eva xx

P.S. I'd really appreciate you leaving a book review, star rating, or your thoughts from the retailer you purchased The Spiritual Nervous System from.

# TWELVE

........................................

# ADDITIONAL RESOURCES

I have created a storefront with additional  and optional resources that were mentioned in this resource. Scan the QR Code to access the storefront for ideas & further reading:

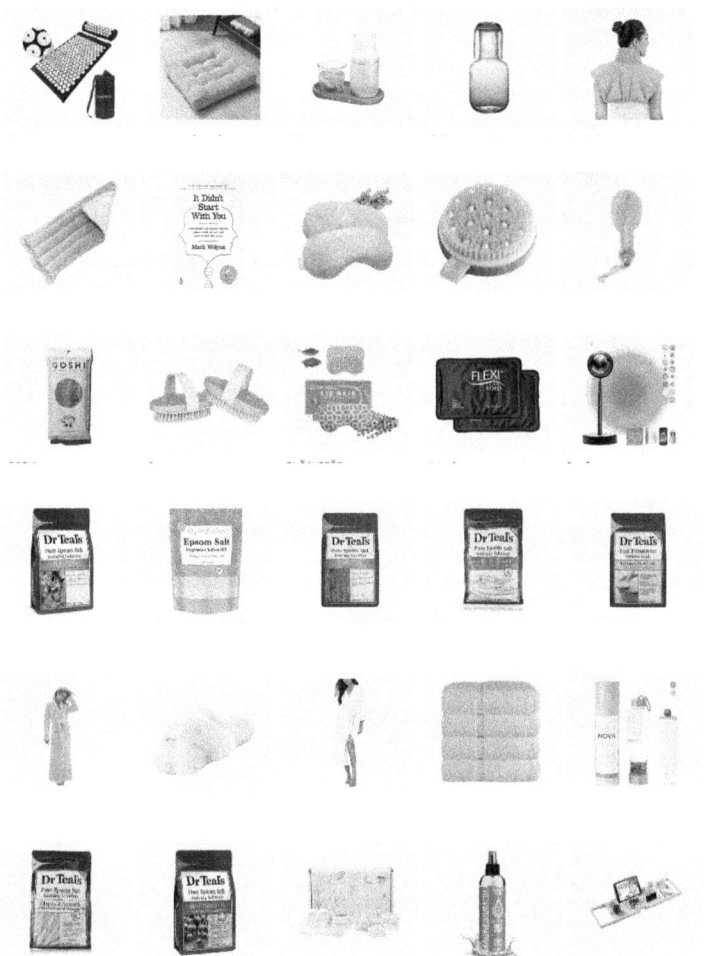

# OTHER BOOKS & JOURNALS
# BY EVA HATTIN

MANIFESTATION

HUMAN DESIGN

GRATITUDE

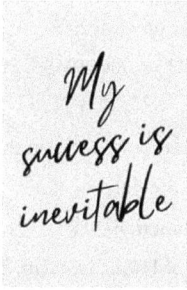

MANTRAS

TAROT & ORACLE

HUMAN DESIGN

GRATITUDE JOURNALS
FOR KIDS

# NOTES

∙∙∙∙∙∙∙∙∙∙∙∙∙∙∙∙∙∙∙∙∙∙∙∙∙∙∙∙∙∙∙

- Cooper-Kahn, J., & Dietzel, L. (n.d.). What is executive functioning? Retrieved from http://www.ldonline.org/article/29122

- Cowen, A. S., Elfenbein, H. A., Laukka, P., & Keltner, D. (2019). Mapping 24 emotions conveyed by brief human vocalization. American Psychologist, 74(6), 698–712. https://doi.org/10.1037/amp0000399

- Dana, D. A. (2021). Anchored. Sounds True, US

- Diamond, A. (2013). Executive Functions. Annual Review of Psychology, 64(1), 135-168. Retrieved from https://www.ncbi.nlm.nih.gov/pmc/articles/PMC4084861

- Frances, A. (2021). Rich as F*ck; More Money Than You Know What to Do With (1st ed.). Amanda Frances Inc.

- Gibbons CH. Basics of autonomic nervous system function. Handb Clin Neurol. 2019;160:407-418. doi: 10.1016/B978-0-444-64032-1.00027-8. PMID: 31277865.

- Guidi J, Lucente M, Sonino N, Fava GA. Allostatic Load and Its Impact on Health: A Systematic Review. Psychother Psychosom. 2021;90(1):11-27. doi: 10.1159/000510696. Epub 2020 Aug 14. PMID: 32799204.

- Harvard University (2015, March 19). Executive Function & Self-Regulation. Center on the Developing Child at Harvard University. Retrieved August 20, 2021, from https://developingchild.harvard.edu/science/key-concepts/executive-function/

- Hu, R. U., & Bunnel, L. (2011). Human Design: The Definitive Book of Human Design, The Science of Differentiation by Ra Uru Hu. HDC Publishing.

- Juster RP, McEwen BS, Lupien SJ. Allostatic load biomarkers of chronic stress and impact on health and cognition. Neurosci Biobehav Rev. 2010 Sep;35(1):2-16. doi: 10.1016/j.neubiorev.2009.10.002. Epub 2009 Oct 12. PMID: 19822172.

- Karemaker JM. An introduction into autonomic nervous function. Physiol Meas. 2017 May;38(5):R89-R118. doi: 10.1088/1361-6579/aa6782. Epub 2017 Mar 17. PMID: 28304283.

- Kok, Bethany & Coffey, Kimberly & Cohn, Michael & Catalino, Lahnna & Vacharkulksemsuk, Tanya & Algoe, Sara & Brantley, Mary & Fredricks=on, Barbara. (2013). How Positive Emotions Build Physical Health: Perceived Positive Social Connections Account for the Upward Spiral Between Positive Emotions and Vagal Tone. Psychological science. 24. 10.1177/0956797612470827.

- Mateos-Aparicio P, Rodríguez-Moreno A. The Impact of Studying Brain Plasticity. Front Cell Neurosci. 2019 Feb 27;13:66. doi: 10.3389/fncel.2019.00066. PMID: 30873009; PMCID: PMC6400842.

- Marc A. Russo, Danielle M. Santarelli, Dean O'Rourke. The physiological effects of slow breathing in the healthy human Breathe Dec 2017, 13 (4) 298-309; DOI: 10.1183/20734735.009817

- Marjorie Beeghly, Ed Tronick, Early Resilience in the Context of Parent–Infant Relationships: A Social Developmental Perspective, Current Problems in Pediatric and Adolescent Health Care, Volume 41, Issue 7, 2011, Pages 197-201, ISSN 1538-5442, https://doi.org/10.1016/j.cppeds.2011.02.005.

- McConnell, S. (2020). Somatic Internal Family Systems Therapy : Awareness, Breath, Resonance, Movement, and Touch in Practice. North Atlantic Books,U.S.

- Mulkey SB, du Plessis AJ. Autonomic nervous system development and its impact on neuropsychiatric outcome. Pediatr Res. 2019 Jan;85(2):120-126. doi: 10.1038/s41390-018-0155-0. Epub 2018 Aug 30. PMID: 30166644; PMCID: PMC6353676.

- Navarro X. Fisiologia del sistema nervioso autónomo [Physiology of the autonomic nervous system]. Rev Neurol. 2002 Sep 16-30;35(6):553-62. Spanish. PMID: 12389173.

- Porges SW. Polyvagal Theory: A Science of Safety. Front Integr Neurosci. 2022 May 10;16:871227. doi: 10.3389/fnint.2022.871227. PMID: 35645742; PMCID: PMC9131189.

- Porges SW. Social engagement and attachment: a phylogenetic perspective. Ann N Y Acad Sci. 2003 Dec;1008:31-47. doi: 10.1196/annals.1301.004. PMID: 14998870.

- Porges SW. The polyvagal perspective. Biol Psychol. 2007 Feb;74(2):116-43. doi: 10.1016/j.biopsycho.2006.06.009. Epub 2006 Oct 16. PMID: 17049418; PMCID: PMC1868418.

- Rosenberg, S. (2017). Accessing the healing power of the vagus nerve: self-help exercises for anxiety, depression, trauma, and autism. Berkeley, California, North Atlantic Books.

- Vitor H Pereira, Isabel Campos, Nuno Sousa, The role of autonomic nervous system in susceptibility and resilience to stress, Current Opinion in Behavioral Sciences, Volume 14, 2017, Pages 102-107, ISSN 2352-1546, https://doi.org/10.1016/j.cobeha.2017.01.003.

- Wehrwein EA, Orer HS, Barman SM. Overview of the Anatomy, Physiology, and Pharmacology of the Autonomic Nervous System. Compr Physiol. 2016 Jun 13;6(3):1239-78. doi: 10.1002/cphy.c150037. PMID: 27347892.

www.ingramcontent.com/pod-product-compliance
Lightning Source LLC
Chambersburg PA
CBHW071858090426

42811CB00004B/655